Your Child's First Teacher *Is You*

Miriam Lukken

Your Child's First Teacher Is You
All Rights Reserved.
Copyright © 2020 Miriam Lukken
v7.0

The opinions expressed in this manuscript are solely the opinions of the author and do not represent the opinions or thoughts of the publisher. The author has represented and warranted full ownership and/or legal right to publish all the materials in this book.

This book may not be reproduced, transmitted, or stored in whole or in part by any means, including graphic, electronic, or mechanical without the express written consent of the publisher except in the case of brief quotations embodied in critical articles and reviews.

Outskirts Press, Inc.
http://www.outskirtspress.com

ISBN: 978-1-9772-1885-8

Cover Photo © 2020 www.gettyimages.com. All rights reserved - used with permission.

Outskirts Press and the "OP" logo are trademarks belonging to Outskirts Press, Inc.

PRINTED IN THE UNITED STATES OF AMERICA

All content in this book is provided for general information only and should not be treated as a substitute for the medical advice of your doctor or healthcare professional. For diagnosis or treatment of any medical problem, consult your own physician. The publisher and author are not responsible for any specific health or allergy needs that may require medical supervision and are not liable for any damages or negative consequences from any treatment, action, application, or preparation to any person reading or following the information in this book. References are provided for informational purposes only and do not constitute an endorsement of any website or other resources. Readers should be aware that the websites listed in this book may change.

The CDC milestone checklists appearing in this book are not a substitute for a standardized, validated developmental screening tool.

Information from **Zero to Three** reprinted with permission.

Your Child's First Teacher Is You, compiled and edited by Miriam Lukken, M.Ed. for BLOCKS: a United Way of West Georgia Initiative.

United Way of West Georgia, 200 Main Street, LaGrange, Georgia 30240

unitedwaywga.org. blockswga.org.

Table of Contents

Introduction i

CHAPTER 1: BIRTH TO ONE YEAR 1
Birth to Three Months 2
Three to Six Months 6
Four-Month-Old Milestones 8
Six-Month-Old Milestones 10
Six to Nine Months 12
Nine-Month-Old Milestones 14
What To Avoid: Screen Time and Secondhand Smoke 16
Nine to Twelve Months 18
One-Year-Old Milestones 21
Teaching Your One-Year-Old 23

CHAPTER 2: 12 TO 24 MONTHS 27
12 to 15 Months 28
15-Month-Old Milestones 30
15 to 18 Months 34
18-Month Milestones 37
18 to 24 Months 39
Teaching Your 18-Month-Old 41
Two-Year-Old Milestones 43

CHAPTER 3: 24 TO 36 MONTHS 47
24 to 30 Months 48
30-Month-Old Milestones 52
Teaching Your Two-Year-Old 55
30 to 36 Months 58
36-Month-Old Milestones 60
Teaching Your Three-Year-Old 62
Digital Media Changes the Brain 67

CHAPTER 4: YOUR FOUR-YEAR-OLD 71
Your Four-Year-Old 72
Four-Year-Old Milestones 76
Teaching Your Four-Year-Old 78

CHAPTER 5: YOUR FIVE-YEAR-OLD **83**
Your Five-Year-Old...84
Five-Year-Old Milestones 86
Teaching Your Five-Year-Old..88
A Kindergarten Readiness Checklist 91

CHAPTER 6: COMMON PARENTING MISTAKES **97**
Common Parenting Mistakes and How to Fix Them 98
Train Their Brain for Success 101

Bibliography **105**

Appendix **107**
Babies Learning On Course for Kindergarten Success 108
Georgia's Babies Can't Wait Program 109

Community Resource Directory **112**
Assistance Programs Services 112
State Licensed Child Care Services in Troup County 115
Community Resource Listing Programs for Children 120
Children's Health Services 123
Community Family Assistance Services 125
Community Food Bank Resources 126
Community Housing Assistance Services 129
Medicaid Enrollment Services 131
Community Shelter Resources...131
Hotline Numbers Resources 134
Suggested Reading 136

Index 137

Introduction

Congratulations on becoming a new parent! You have just begun one of the most rewarding experiences you will ever have in life.

As you already know, being a parent is not without its challenges. But with a little knowledge, you can prepare your child to be the very best version of himself and set him on a course for a lifetime of success and achievement. All it takes is a little effort and attention from you, his very first teacher.

The book you hold in your hands can help you along the way.

You'll learn:

- what to expect at each age of your child's development
- milestones to look out for at each age
- what you can do to make your baby healthier and smarter
- age-appropriate activities for each stage of your child's development
- a list of resources for help, support, and further information

Did you know that **the first three years of a child's life are uniquely important? This is the most sensitive period for brain development.**

People often assume that because children cannot remember the first year of life, early experiences don't really matter to a baby. But that is simply not true.

A child's brain develops 80% of its capacity by the time he reaches the age of three.

A baby will learn more at this time period than at any other period in his life.

By age five, children's brains have developed 90% of their capacity.

But many parents assume their child's education starts at kindergarten, when actually, **it starts the moment you hold your baby in your arms.**

Why? Because **early experiences matter.** Years of research have confirmed what parents have always known by instinct: **that everyday moments, showing affection, comforting, and playing with young children is exactly what is needed to help build strong, healthy brains.**

This is why it is so important for you to talk to, sing to, and read to your baby <u>from the very beginning.</u>

It's the quality of a baby's relationships that has a major influence on which brain connections take place and the strength of these connections.

What does this mean?

From the moment of birth, supportive relationships in the early years plant the seeds for **love, safety,** and **security,** which **forge a very important set of connections in the brain** that help children learn and bond with others.

The brains of children who don't experience love, safety, and meaningful interaction from their parents are wired to sense danger and to respond to threat. This increases children's anxiety, fear, and feelings of insecurity, which interferes with learning.

A baby's brain connections reflect the quality of the care they receive.

These differences have impacts that can last a lifetime: our brain connections affect the way we think, the way we learn, and the way we manage our feelings and build relationships with others all the way into adulthood.

So what does your baby need to build healthy brain connections?

She needs **YOU** to **tune in to her signals, her words, her facial expressions, and her actions and respond in ways that respect her individual needs.**

We call this **RESPONSIVE CARE, and it can actually make your baby smarter!**

When you respond in this sensitive way, you are letting your child know you understand what she's telling you, and that you respect her needs. These loving back-and-forth interactions build strong, positive brain connections that help your child thrive over time.

REMEMBER: <u>You cannot spoil your baby during his first six months!</u>

He needs all your love, comfort, and understanding every day for his brain to make important connections that will benefit him for the rest of his life.

Babies who are securely attached to someone special during their first year do better in school, work, and relationships for the rest of their lives.

How else can you nurture healthy brain connection?

By seeing your child as a partner in your interactions. Like a game of catch, **it's all about back-and-forth. One of you starts the interaction, the other responds.**

You talk to your baby, then give him time to respond; with sounds, words, or actions. Then you answer back. **It's a dialogue.**

The most important thing a child needs to thrive is an environment of positive, engaging, loving, and caring relationships with adults, including family members and childcare providers.[1]

Did you know that six **out of ten children enter kindergarten unprepared?**

But your child will be ready if you follow this simple, ongoing reference guide!

In the following pages you will find lots of simple and inexpensive ways to nurture your baby's growth and help your child develop the necessary skills that will be critical as he grows up and enters school:

- **thinking**
- **self-control**
- **self-confidence**

But most importantly, he will develop **a love for you, and a love for learning**.

---

[1] Zero to Three; Brain Development from Birth, 2013

A WARNING ABOUT BABIES AND CELL PHONES

Babies learn by interacting. When you're feeding him, your face is the perfect distance for him to be able to focus on you. He'll learn everything about you—the most important person in his world. He'll be fascinated by your eyes, your smile, your voice.

- When you hold his gaze, you're teaching him to pay attention.
- Whenever you talk to him, you're helping his little brain learn our tricky language.
- And as you interact with him for those few minutes, you and baby are strengthening your bond.

Words can't express how much your baby values your undivided attention, even if it's just rubbing his head and cooing to him while his eyes are closed.

While you're giving baby your undivided attention, you'll notice his nursing patterns.

Does he struggle and gag a bit when your milk lets down? Perhaps your letdown is a bit overwhelming and a different position would be helpful for him.

Does he tend to get drowsy five minutes into feeding?

You can stop that from happening by tickling his toes and blowing on his hair four minutes into his feeding.

Does he need to burp partway through a feeding?

Maybe he just loses interest after a little while and starts looking around the room to see what else is out there.

These are all things you probably won't notice if you're looking at your cell phone.

Experts believe that cell phone usage while breastfeeding can lead to emotional and relationship issues among babies.

Eye contact with your baby while he's breastfeeding is so important because it helps the brain develop in healthy ways. **If your baby is trying to make contact with you through staring, facial expressions, hand gestures, noises, or smiles and you are distracted by your cell phone, your baby will not be able to establish the deep emotional bond with you.** You will miss the subtle cues that your baby sends you.

If babies learn that they can't rely on you to respond to them, it will affect their sense of trust, comfort, and security that they generally associate with their mother. Such things can affect the child's psyche in the long term. They may start feeling neglected, which can make them anxious and irritable. With time, it can lead to other issues such as sleep deprivation, depression, and improper diet. **Since eye contact with your baby is so important, and lack of it can lead to long term issues, it is advised that you minimize cell phone usage while breastfeeding, or better yet, avoid it all together.**

Protect your baby from cell phone radiation

Many people don't realize that cell phones and tablets are dangerous to kids and especially babies. They emit microwave radiation, and the closer a baby is, the more their little body absorbs.

This isn't the same kind of radiation that your microwave emits—that kind is continuous. The radiation from phones and tablets is intermittent, and it can damage brain cells, cause cancer and other diseases, disrupt a baby's DNA structure, and weaken the brain's protective barrier. A five-year-old's brain, healthy or otherwise, is encased in a thinner skull and contains more fluid than an adult brain. The bone marrow of a child's head absorbs ten times more radiation than an adult, while that of infants and toddlers will absorb even more.[2]

For WIC participants who need help breastfeeding, call 706-298-6080 or 770-722-0633 to be connected to a Peer Counselor or Lactation Consultant.

---

[2] healthychild.org. According to the World Health Organization, cell phone radiation is a Class 2 B carcinogen. That's the same classification as DDT, lead, and jet fuel.

CHAPTER 1

BIRTH TO ONE YEAR

Birth to Three Months

The first three months are all about babies learning to **feel safe, comfortable, and secure.** By responding to their signals and providing lots of love and comfort, you help your baby form a trusting bond with you.

How are you helping your baby learn to feel safe and secure?

What Your Baby Can Do	What You Can Do
I am getting to know you and the other people who love and care for me. * I recognize faces, voices, and smells. * I respond to your smile and touch with pleasure.	**Talk and sing to your baby.** This makes him feel loved and helps him bond with you. **Hold your baby.** Enjoy some skin-to-skin cuddle time with your baby.
I am learning how to "tell" you what I need. * I can use sounds, expressions, and movement to tell you if I am sleepy, hungry, happy, or uncomfortable. * I can show you when I want to play, or need a break.	**Watch your baby to learn her signals.** Does she have a "hunger" cry? Does she rub her eyes or look away from you when she is tired? **Respond to your baby's signals.** When her eyes are bright and she is alert and awake, it is time to play. Slow things down when she cries, turns away, or arches her back.
I am beginning to use my body to make things happen. * I can grip your finger or a toy you put in my hand. * When I'm hungry, I might move my head toward my mother's breast or the bottle.	**Give your baby something to reach for and hold onto—a finger or a toy.** Watch to see how your baby is discovering his body. Does he look at his hand, suck on his feet, or try to roll?
We are becoming closer and closer every day. * I am learning to trust that you will read and respond to my signals. * I rely on you to comfort me. This helps me to comfort myself.	**Comfort your baby whenever she cries.** You cannot spoil a baby. Soothing makes her feel safe, secure, and loved. **Help your baby calm herself** by guiding her fingers to her mouth, giving her a pacifier, or offering her a blanket or soft object that is special to her.

About Crying: Crying is normal and the way babies communicate hunger, distress, or a need for your attention. Most newborns reach a crying peak at about six weeks. By three months they typically cry for about an hour a day.

Being with a crying baby can be stressful and frustrating, but by holding and comforting your baby, you are teaching him that he is not alone and that you love him.

All babies cry, but some cry much more than others. This is known as **colic**, which is defined as crying that:

- begins and ends for no obvious reason
- lasts at least three hours a day
- happens at least three days a week
- continues for three weeks to three months.

Tips on Soothing Your Baby's Crying:

Try holding your baby more. Some babies cry less when they are held more. Wrap your baby snuggly in a blanket—called "swaddling"—and rock her gently.

Use soothing sounds. Talk or sing softly to your baby. Try running a fan or humidifier in your baby's room. Sometimes babies are soothed by this background noise.

Reduce stimulation. Lights, sights, sounds, and textures can cause your baby to cry. Sometimes less stimulation leads to less crying for babies with colic.

Reach out for support. Extended families and friends may be able to step in to give you a needed break. Everyone needs support, and nobody needs it more than the parents of a crying baby.

Stay calm. When you're calm, it helps your baby calm down. If you find yourself feeling frustrated, put your baby on his back in a safe place, like a crib, and take a short break. Crying won't hurt your baby, and taking a break will let you soothe another very important person—you!

Talk with your healthcare provider. Crying may have a medical cause—a food sensitivity, heartburn, or other physical condition.

Don't give up. Soothing your baby is a trial-and-error process. If one strategy doesn't work, try another. Hang in there, and remember that the crying will get better.

Teaching Your Baby:

The way you respond to your baby helps nurture his brain. When you answer his cries, he learns to communicate with you more, first through sounds and movement and later through words. Try these activities to encourage him:

Talk and sing to your baby. This is one of <u>the most important things you can do</u> to help your baby's brain development.

Tell him about everything that's going on around him. As you are feeding him, changing his diaper, or getting him dressed, just tell him what you are doing.

Pay attention to the sights and sounds he likes. Find toys and everyday objects with different colors and textures and see which one he likes best. Offer your baby lots of different objects for him to look at, touch, and even grip in his fingers and hands. He can focus best on things that are eight to ten inches away.

Play tracking games by moving yourself and interesting objects back and forth. First he will use his eyes to follow. Eventually he will move his head from side to side. This helps strengthen his neck and eye muscles.[3]

Fever in Infants

A fever is a common sign of illness in children. A raised temperature is a normal response to an infection caused by bacteria (germ) or a virus. A child's normal temperature ranges from 97°F to 99°F. In most cases, a fever is not dangerous, but in young infants it can be very serious. If your child has a fever and is younger than three months old, talk to your child's doctor right away.

How to take a newborn's temperature:

The most accurate way to take a baby's temperature is in his bottom. Other methods are not as accurate. Always use a digital thermometer. Do not use a glass, temporal (forehead), or pacifier thermometer as those can be less accurate.

1. Lay your baby on his stomach across your lap or in his crib. Keep one hand on his back to hold him safely. You also can lay your baby on his back and lift up his legs like you do when you change his diaper.
2. Dip the tip of the thermometer in Vaseline (petroleum jelly).
3. Turn on the thermometer.
4. Put it 1/2 to 1 inch into your baby's bottom. Hold it in place.
5. Listen for the signal or beep.
6. Remove the thermometer.
7. Read the number and write it down.

---

[3] www.zerotothree.org reprinted with permission.

When to see a doctor:

Call your baby's doctor if:

- He has a rectal temperature over 100.3°F and is younger than three months old.
- He has a rectal temperature over 102.2°F and is 3 to 24 months old.
- He has an underlying chronic medical condition or has other signs such as a new rash, poor feeding, frequent vomiting, diarrhea, severe cough, or difficulty breathing in addition to the fever.
- He has a change in behavior.
- He does not wake up easily.
- He does not feel well.
- He falls or is burned.
- He vomits more than two times in one hour.
- He has less than one wet diaper every 4 to 6 hours or less than 5 to 6 wet diapers in 24 hours.
- He has blood in his urine or bowel movement.

Fever Tips:

Encourage your child to play if he feels like it.

Remove extra layers of clothing.

Make sure your child drinks plenty of fluids.

Place a cool cloth on his head to help him feel more comfortable.

Never give your child aspirin or aspirin products.

Ask your doctor about medicines before giving them to your child.

A fever after receiving a vaccine is usually not dangerous.

If the fever gets higher than 102°F, or if you are concerned about your baby, call his doctor.

Trust your instincts.

Three to Six Months

This time is all about parents and babies falling in love. Most babies are eating and sleeping more regularly. They are also responding more actively to parents and caregivers. Over the next few months, you will begin learning about your baby's preferences—what he likes and dislikes, how he prefers to sleep, eat, and play.

What are you learning about your little one?

What Your Baby Can Do	What You Can Do
I am learning to control my body. * I push myself up to see the people I love and the things that interest me. I roll to try to get closer to you or to an interesting toy or object. * I can sit with help and hold my head steady. * I may start to rock back and forth on my hands and knees to get ready to crawl so I can get moving and explore.	**Place your baby in different positions to help her develop new skills like rolling, creeping, and crawling.** * Make sure she gets time to play on both her back and stomach. * Help her sit with support. This allows her to explore in new ways. * Be sure she is always put to sleep on her back.
I use my hands and fingers to explore. * I reach for and grasp objects and toys. I explore them with my fingers, hands, and mouth to figure out what they can do.	**Offer your baby toys to explore** that have different shapes, sizes, textures, and sounds. Show him ways to use these objects by shaking, banging, pushing, and dropping.
I can communicate by using sounds, actions, and facial expressions. * When you shake my rattle, I may smile and move my arms and legs to let you know I want to keep playing. * I can make a few different sounds in response to your sounds—babbles, coos, and gurgles.	**Watch and respond to your baby's signals.** * *You are smiling, I think you like looking in the mirror. Do you want to look at yourself again?* **Have back-and-forth conversations with your baby.** When you reply to her babbles, she knows you care about what she is saying. This helps her learn to talk.
I am getting used to the world around me. * I may be starting to develop a more regular eating and sleeping schedule. * I am beginning to notice daily routines. When you turn the lights down, I am learning it is time for sleep.	**Create routines for your baby.** * Help him learn it's time for sleep by doing the same things in the same order each night, such as bath, books, feeding, and then a lullaby. * Make up a song that you sing as you are getting ready to feed your baby. Each time he hears it, he will know milk is coming. This may calm him and also help him learn to wait.

Learning Language

Babies are not just listeners; they are talkers too. Beginning at about two to three months, they use their voices to coo, laugh, and squeal. And even young babies are learning the rules of conversation. As early as three to four months, babies will stay quiet while someone else is talking. They wait for silence, then babble, then wait for your response.

By about six months, babies begin to repeat certain sounds like mama or dada. Around one year they make the connection in their minds between a sound they make—*baba*—and the object it stands for—*bottle*. After they make this link, your baby's use of words really starts to grow!

Teaching Your Baby:

Sing to your baby. Singing lets children hear and later repeat words and phrases. It's also a great way to have fun and bond with your baby.

Read to your baby. Reading together at this age builds a love of books. Don't make the mistake of thinking babies are too young to read to. **Reading to your baby is the single most important thing you can do to ensure success at school.**

Notice and respond to your baby's signals. This helps your baby develop stronger thinking and social-emotional skills. **Responding to your baby's cries and meeting his needs is not spoiling him—it's being a great parent.** The following three steps can help you understand what your baby is telling you before he can talk:

1. **Watch and listen.** Look for patterns in his cries, sounds, facial expressions, and body movements. For example, does your baby suck her fingers when she's hungry?
2. **Understand.** Use your child's signals to figure out what he needs or wants. For example, your baby may rub his eyes when he is sleepy.
3. **Respond.** You might take a break from playing when she arches her back and looks away. Keep in mind that you may have to try several different responses before you figure out exactly what she needs or is trying to communicate.[4]

---

4   www.zerotothree.org reprinted with permission.

Four-Month-Old Milestones

Milestones matter! How your child plays, learns, speaks, acts, and moves offers important clues about his or her development. Check the milestones your child has reached by four months. As you use this resource, remember that your child may develop skills faster or slower than indicated here and still be growing just fine. Premature babies may meet milestones a little later than full-term babies. Take this with you and talk with your child's doctor at every well-child visit about the milestones your child has reached and what to expect next.

Social/Emotional

- ☐ Smiles spontaneously, especially at people
- ☐ Likes to play with people and might cry when playing stops
- ☐ Copies some movements and facial expressions, like smiling or frowning

Language/Communication

- ☐ Begins to babble
- ☐ Babbles with expression and copies sounds he hears
- ☐ Cries in different ways to show hunger, pain, or being tired

Cognitive (learning, thinking, problem-solving)

- ☐ Lets you know if she is happy or sad
- ☐ Responds to affection
- ☐ Reaches for toy with one hand
- ☐ Uses hands and eyes together, such as seeing a toy and reaching for it
- ☐ Follows moving things with eyes from side to side
- ☐ Watches faces closely
- ☐ Recognizes familiar people and things at a distance

Movement/Physical Development

- ☐ Holds head steady, unsupported
- ☐ Pushes down on legs when feet are on a hard surface
- ☐ May be able to roll over from tummy to back
- ☐ Can hold a toy and shake it and swing at dangling toys
- ☐ Brings hands to mouth
- ☐ When lying on stomach, pushes up to elbows

BIRTH TO ONE YEAR

You know your child best. Act early if you have concerns about the way your child plays, learns, speaks, acts, or moves, or if your child:

- ☐ Is missing milestones
- ☐ Doesn't watch things as they move
- ☐ Doesn't smile at people
- ☐ Can't hold head steady
- ☐ Doesn't coo or make sounds
- ☐ Doesn't bring things to mouth
- ☐ Doesn't push down with legs when feet are placed on a hard surface
- ☐ Has trouble moving one or both eyes in all directions

Tell your child's doctor or nurse if you notice any of these signs of possible developmental delay and ask for a developmental screening.

If you or the doctor is still concerned:

Ask for a referral to a specialist and call your state's early intervention program to find out if your child can get services to help. Learn more and find the number at **cdc.gov/FindEI**.

For more information, go to **cdc.gov/Concerned**.

*This milestone CDC checklist is not a substitute for a standardized, validated developmental screening tool.

Six-Month-Old Milestones

Milestones matter! How your child plays, learns, speaks, acts, and moves offers important clues about his or her development. Check the milestones your child has reached by six months. As you use this resource, remember that your child may develop skills faster or slower than indicated here and still be growing just fine. Premature babies may meet milestones a little later than full-term babies. Take this with you and talk with your child's doctor at every well-child visit about the milestones your child has reached and what to expect next.

Social/Emotional

- ☐ Knows familiar faces and begins to know if someone is a stranger
- ☐ Likes to play with others, especially parents
- ☐ Responds to other people's emotions and often seems happy
- ☐ Likes to look at self in a mirror

Language/Communication

- ☐ Responds to sounds by making sounds
- ☐ Strings vowels together when babbling ("ah," "eh," "oh") and likes taking turns with parent while making sounds
- ☐ Responds to own name
- ☐ Makes sounds to show joy and displeasure
- ☐ Begins to say consonant sounds (jabbering with "m," "b")

Cognitive (learning, thinking, problem-solving)

- ☐ Looks around at things nearby
- ☐ Brings things to mouth
- ☐ Shows curiosity about things and tries to get things that are out of reach
- ☐ Begins to pass things from one hand to the other

Movement/Physical Development

- ☐ Rolls over in both directions (front to back, back to front)
- ☐ Begins to sit without support
- ☐ When standing, supports weight on legs and might bounce
- ☐ Rocks back and forth, sometimes crawling backward before moving forward

BIRTH TO ONE YEAR

You know your child best. Act early if you have concerns about the way your child plays, learns, speaks, acts, or moves, or if your child:

- ☐ Is missing milestones
- ☐ Doesn't try to get things that are in reach
- ☐ Shows no affection for caregivers
- ☐ Doesn't respond to sounds around him
- ☐ Has difficulty getting things to mouth
- ☐ Doesn't make vowel sounds (ah, eh, oh)
- ☐ Doesn't roll over in either direction
- ☐ Doesn't laugh or make squealing sounds
- ☐ Seems very stiff, with tight muscles
- ☐ Seems very floppy, like a rag doll

Tell your child's doctor or nurse if you notice any of these signs of possible developmental delay and ask for a developmental screening.

If you or the doctor is still concerned:

Ask for a referral to a specialist and call your state's intervention program to find out if your child can get services to help. Learn more and find the number at **cdc.gov/FindEI**.

For more information, go to **cdc.gov/Concerned**.

*This milestone checklist is not a substitute for a standardized, validated developmental screening tool.

Six to Nine Months

This is a time of great fun for parents as they watch their babies become eager explorers who are thrilled to discover that they can make things happen. A seven-month-old knows, *When I smile, Mommy smiles back!* A nine-month-old lifts her arms to tell her father, *I want you to pick me up.*

How is your baby making things happen?

What Your Baby Can Do	What You Can Do
I am learning to think and solve problems. * When a toy drops to the floor, I look to see where it went. * I figure out how things work by copying what I see you and others do.	**Comment on what your baby does to make things happen.** *You used your voice to let me know you wanted me to keep playing peekaboo.* **Let your baby explore interesting objects:** like toys with buttons to push.
I can control my body. * I can pick up small objects using my thumb and other fingers. * I can sit on my own, which helps me explore in new ways. * I may crawl or scoot to get around. I might even pull up on furniture to stand.	**Begin letting your child practice picking up baby-safe foods like slices of banana,** if you'd like your child to learn to feed himself. **Give your baby time to move around on his own.** This builds muscle strength and coordination.
I am working hard to communicate with you. * I babble a lot. When someone talks to me, I make sounds back. * I use my voice to express feelings, like joy and anger. * I copy actions you make, like waving *"Bye-bye"* and shaking my head *"no-no."*	**Use words to describe your baby's feelings.** *You are mad that Daddy took away the crayon; you can chew on this rattle instead.* **If your baby is looking at something, point at it and explain:** *That's a radio. It plays music.* **Copy your baby's sounds and actions.** If she waves, wave back and say *hello!*
My personality is starting to show. * I may love to meet new people or need time to feel comfortable with someone I don't know yet. * I may like lots of sound and activity or I may prefer things to be more quiet and calm. * I may be very active or more interested in just watching.	**Notice how your baby likes to play and explore.** Does she like to move or does she prefer to sit and watch the world around her? **See how your baby reacts to sounds, sights, and social activity.** What does she seem to enjoy? What does she seem to dislike or get overwhelmed by?

Helping Your Baby Learn to Sleep Through the Night

By six months, most full-term, healthy babies are able to sleep through the night. If you'd like your baby to learn this skill, it's important to be patient and consistent with how you handle bedtime and night wakings. This helps your baby learn to soothe himself and go back to sleep more easily and quickly.

Teach Your Baby:

Use a bedtime routine. Loving and relaxing bedtime routines—like a bath, story, milk, teeth cleaning, and then lullaby—help babies settle down and learn when it's time to go to sleep. Just be sure not to leave a cup or bottle in the crib or bed. Not only will your child come to depend on having a bottle to get to sleep, but leaving a bottle in your sleeping baby's mouth can cause tooth decay.

Put your baby to bed while he's sleepy but still awake. We all wake up to some degree during the night as we move through different stages of sleep. If children are fed or comforted by a loved one to fall asleep, when they wake up in the middle of the night, they depend on that same kind of comfort to fall back to sleep. When you put your baby down sleepy but awake, he learns how to fall asleep on his own.

Plan for protests. Make a plan for what to do if your baby cries while she is learning to fall asleep. Some parents choose to check on their child several times until she falls asleep. Other parents say a clear good night and do not return until morning. (For some children having their parents come in and out can make it harder for them to calm down and fall asleep.) But if you do go to her at night to reassure her you are still there, don't pick her up and rock her back to sleep. Falling asleep in your arms makes it more difficult for her to soothe herself back to sleep if she wakes up again at night. There is not just one right way to help babies learn to sleep through the night. Try different routines until you find what works best for your baby, and remember to trust your instincts.

Your baby is watching and learning through you. At this age, babies begin to look to loved ones for clues about how to feel about a situation. For example, when a new person comes to the house, a baby looks to his parents to see how they respond: *Are they smiling and happy? Is this person okay? Can I trust him?* To help your baby adjust when meeting a new person, show with your own face, voice, and actions that he or she is nice and trustworthy.

Separation Anxiety

Starting around eight or nine months, babies may become upset and fearful when separated from a loved one. This happens because babies are beginning to understand that people still exist even when they can't see them. So they naturally protest to try to make their special person stay. To help your baby adjust to separations, read stories about saying goodbye (like *Owl Babies* by Martin Waddell). And use a goodbye routine with your baby each time you leave, like a song, a kiss, and a big wave. **Routines help babies feel safe.** To help your child make the transition to her caregiver, suggest that the three of you play with one of your child's favorite toys or books before you leave. Most importantly, be sure to say a real goodbye to your baby. Sneaking out makes babies worry that you may disappear at any time without warning. This makes separation even harder and can create feelings of mistrust.[5]

---

[5] www.zerotothree.org reprinted with permission.

Nine-Month-Old Milestones

Milestones matter! How your child plays, learns, speaks, acts, and moves offers important clues about his or her development. Check the milestones your child has reached by nine months. As you use this resource, remember that your child may develop skills faster or slower than indicated here and still be growing just fine. Premature babies may meet milestones a little later than full-term babies. Take this with you and talk with your child's doctor at every well-child visit about the milestones your child has reached and what to expect next.

Social/Emotional

- ☐ May be afraid of strangers
- ☐ May be clingy with familiar adults
- ☐ Has favorite toys

Language/Communication

- ☐ Understands "no"
- ☐ Makes a lot of different sounds like "mamamama" and "bababababa"
- ☐ Copies sounds and gestures of others
- ☐ Uses fingers to point at things

Cognitive (learning, thinking, problem-solving)

- ☐ Watches the path of something as it falls
- ☐ Looks for things he sees you hide
- ☐ Plays peek-a-boo
- ☐ Puts things in her mouth
- ☐ Moves things smoothly from one hand to the other
- ☐ Picks up things like cereal o's between thumb and index finger

Movement/Physical Development

- ☐ Stands, holding on
- ☐ Can get into sitting position
- ☐ Sits without support
- ☐ Pulls to stand
- ☐ Crawls

BIRTH TO ONE YEAR

Act early if you have concerns about the way your child plays, learns, speaks, acts, or moves, or if your child:

- ☐ Is missing milestones
- ☐ Doesn't bear weight on legs with support
- ☐ Doesn't sit with help
- ☐ Doesn't babble ("mama," "baba," "dada")
- ☐ Doesn't play any games involving back-and-forth play
- ☐ Doesn't respond to own name
- ☐ Doesn't seem to recognize familiar people
- ☐ Doesn't look where you point
- ☐ Doesn't transfer toys from one hand to the other

Tell your child's doctor or nurse if you notice any of these signs of possible developmental delay and ask for a developmental screening.

If you or the doctor is still concerned:

Ask for a referral to a specialist and call your state's early intervention program to find out if your child can get services to help. Learn more and find the number at **cdc.gov/FindEI**. For more information, go to **cdc.gov/Concerned**.

*This milestone CDC checklist is not a substitute for a standardized, validated developmental screening tool.

What To Avoid: Screen Time and Secondhand Smoke

New Screen-Time Recommendations for Children Under Six

The **American Academy of Pediatrics** has recommendations for children's use of "screen media." Here's what the Academy says is best for each age:

- **Birth through 18 months: <u>Avoid all screen media—phones, tablets, TVs, and computers.</u>** (It's okay to video chat with grandparents and faraway friends.)
- **18 months to 2 years:** It is okay to introduce young children to high-quality children's media if you watch it with them and help them understand what they're seeing.
- **2 to 5 years: Limit screen use to one hour a day of high-quality programs (such as *Sesame Street*) designed for children.** Watch with your children; explain what they're seeing and how it applies to the world around them.

Studies Show Parents Should Avoid Screen Time For Children Under Two

A 2017 study found that **the screen time of children under two years old is linked to delays in learning basic expressive speech as a toddler.**

Doctors are blaming the loss of basic motor skills on the changing culture among parents who rely heavily on technology. It's easier to give a child an iPad than encourage them to do muscle-building play such as building blocks. But children need lots of opportunity to develop those skills. Children are not coming to school with the hand strength they had ten years ago. Many don't know how to hold a pencil because they don't have the fundamental movement skills.

Avoid Cell Phone Distracted Parenting

A new study published in *Time Magazine* shows that **cell phone distracted parenting can have long-term consequences on a child's development and detrimental effects on babies' development, especially their ability to process pleasure**.

The study found that just like with sensory systems such as sight and hearing, there may be a critical window in which newborns need to be exposed to certain behaviors from Mom in order for their nervous system to develop properly.

Babies need rhythms and consistent exposure beyond the ears for them to be capable of discerning complex patterns in speech and music. They need patterns for the visual system to develop. They need predictability and consistency for the emotional system to develop.

That means that there is a critical time during which babies need to have a mom and dad's reliable and consistent attention in order to form proper emotional processes. That includes knowing that at a certain time every day, for example, food will come, or that when a toy appears, Mom will play. **If Mom is distracted by a call or a message alert and turns to the cell phone instead, then this pattern gets broken and the crucial learning that should occur might not happen.**

Other studies have shown that such poor development of the pleasure system could contribute to mood disorders such as depression and anxiety.

So there is a sensitive period in which a mother's care needs to provide consistent patterns and sequences of behavior **so the baby's brain can perceive them to develop normally emotionally**.

In order for children to learn to speak, reason, and develop crucial social skills, they need face-to-face interaction with loving people and they need to use all their senses as often as they can.

That's why the American Academy of Pediatrics recommends **kids under age two explore their world without interruption by a screen**, except for the occasional FaceTime with Grandma.

In short, avoid giving your baby access to electronics, even your smartphone, and definitely do not give an iPad to a child under the age of five.

Secondhand Smoke Harms Children and Adults

- There is no risk-free level of secondhand smoke exposure; even brief exposure can be harmful to health.
- Since 1964, approximately 2,500,000 nonsmokers have died from health problems caused by exposure to secondhand smoke.
- Remember that when you smoke in your car with your children, you may be harming their long-term health.

Secondhand Smoke Health Effects in Children

In children, secondhand smoke causes the following:

- Ear infections
- More frequent and severe asthma attacks
- Respiratory symptoms (for example, coughing, sneezing, and shortness of breath)
- Respiratory infections (bronchitis and pneumonia)
- A greater risk for sudden infant death syndrome (SIDS)[6]

---

6 Center for Disease Control and Prevention, Smoking and Tobacco Use, cdc.gov

Nine to Twelve Months

Babies are becoming good communicators as they get closer to turning one year old. This makes it a delightful time for parents. Babies can use their actions and sounds to let loved ones know what they want, like handing a book to a parent so that she'll read it out loud.

How does your baby tell you what he wants?

What Your Baby Can Do	What You Can Do
I can understand more words than I say. * I am starting to understand what you say to me. I can even follow simple directions like *Go get the ball*. * I tell you what I want with my sounds and body movements. * I may say a word or two, like *mama*.	**Tell your baby what is happening and what you will do next:** *After your milk, it is time for a nap.* This helps her learn language. Routines also let her know what to expect. **Put your baby's sounds and actions into words.** *You are pushing your food away. I think you are telling me you are all done.* **Name things your baby looks at and points to:** *That's the moon. The moon comes out at night.*
I can creep and crawl. * I have found my own way of crawling—on my hands or knees, on my stomach, "crab crawling" by moving backward and sideways, or even scooting on my bottom. * I walk while holding onto furniture or your hand. * I may even start walking on my own.	**Give your baby lots of time and a safe place to practice new skills** like crawling and walking. **Make a trail of toys in a child-safe place in your house.** Line up several interesting objects (a wooden spoon, a plastic bowl, a brightly colored dish cloth) that your child can crawl to and explore.
I know that things still exist even though I can't see them—especially you! * I may cry when you leave because I know you are still out there somewhere and I want you to come back!	**Play hide-and-seek games.** This helps your baby learn that things that disappear also reappear. **Be sure to say goodbye to your baby.** Never sneak out. This builds his trust in you and helps him learn to deal with difficult feelings.
I love to do things over and over again. * This is how I practice and figure out how things work. * Repetition also helps build my memory.	**Help your child take the next step in her play.** If she is banging two blocks together, see if she would like to try stacking them. **Offer your child a ball to toss, a rattle to shake, or a scarf to swing.** These activities help children learn how things work. They also build the muscles in their hands that will help them learn to write.

BIRTH TO ONE YEAR

How Babies Connect Their Thoughts and Actions

Between nine and twelve months, babies take action with a goal in mind. For example, your child may crawl off as fast as he can when he sees you holding a clean diaper. He doesn't want a diaper change, so he crawls away to avoid it! **It's important to understand that babies don't do this to make us angry.** They simply want to make their needs and feelings known. These purposeful actions also show that babies have developed a better memory. They remember that they don't like lying still or feeling those cold, wet wipes!

Developing Memory

Between nine and twelve months, your baby is developing a better memory. She can now imitate something she has seen others do—like chat on the phone. Your baby is also learning how objects are supposed to be used. From watching you, she knows a phone is for talking. One way you help your child figure out how the world works is by letting her play with safe objects—like a hairbrush or sponge—and talk about how they look and feel and what they do.

Teaching Your Baby:

Read or tell stories together every day, starting at birth. Read from a book, simply talk about the pictures, or make up stories based on what you see. Have your child point to familiar objects, numbers, or colors. This is how your child learns language. **Remember that 80% of your baby's brain is formed by the age of three.** When you read together, you are helping your child's brain cells make important connections that will last a lifetime.

Teach new words anytime you can. Talk to your child about what you see around you and what you are doing. *"It's very cold outside today, so let's put on your jacket."* The more you speak, the more you build your child's vocabulary.

Sing songs and nursery rhymes over and over again. Add songs and rhymes into all of your routines; sing "Rock-a-Bye Baby" at bedtime and "Rub-a-Dub-Dub" at bath time. Teach him simple songs like "Twinkle, Twinkle, Little Star" and the alphabet song. You can find many more songs at **newkidscenter.org.**

Ask questions and watch for their responses. From day one, ask your child **where** and **what** whenever you can—at the store, on a walk, while looking at pictures or reading stories. Ask questions about **yesterday**, **today,** and **tomorrow**. When you and your child take turns talking and listening, your child is learning to tell the difference between sounds. Later, he will put the sounds together into words.

Show your child how cause-and-effect works, like letting her press the doorbell or turn on the light switch.

Follow your baby's lead. Notice what your baby is interested in and let him (safely) explore an object in his own way. **When a child is engaged and having fun playing, he is learning.** Offer new challenges as your child masters new skills—like suggesting he try to stack more blocks on top of his three-block tower.

Encourage your baby to use all her senses to learn. Let her touch an ice cube. Notice when it melts. Crinkle leaves in your hands and see what happens. Let her shake a plastic container of dry rice and one full of dried beans. How do they sound different?

Childproof yet again! Now that babies have a goal in mind, like touching the television remote, they are harder to distract. Make your home child-safe so you spend more time playing and less time saying *No*!

Use play to introduce language. Give your child books, musical instruments, and other toys. Play hide-and-seek, talking about what you see as you look. When you interact with your child in a playful way, you introduce new words, sounds, and concepts.

The more parents respond to their one-year-olds during play time—showing their own enjoyment and excitement in their child's play and noticing what their child is interested in—the better their child's language skills are at age two.

Behavior

Help your baby handle her feelings. Comfort her when she cries, acknowledge when she's frustrated, and help her calm down and try again. This helps your child manage her very strong feelings and develop self-control.

In response to unwanted behaviors, say "no" firmly. Do not yell, spank, or give long explanations. A time-out for thirty seconds to one minute might help redirect your child.

Spend a lot more time encouraging wanted behaviors than punishing unwanted behaviors. Try for **four times as much encouragement for wanted behaviors** as redirection for unwanted behaviors.

Caregiver tip: Give your child time to get to know a new caregiver. Bring a favorite toy, stuffed animal, or blanket to help comfort your child. Thanks to their new memory skills, babies this age know that when you leave, you still exist. This is a very important skill, but also can lead to difficulty when leaving. Be positive when leaving her. When saying goodbye, tell her you will miss her, but you will return. Make sure she has something that gives her comfort, like her blanket or favorite stuffed toy.[7]

---

7   www.zerotothree.org reprinted with permission.

One-Year-Old Milestones

How your child plays, learns, speaks, acts, and moves offers important clues about his or her development. Check the milestones your child has reached by his first birthday. As you use this resource, remember that your child may develop skills faster or slower than indicated here and still be growing just fine. Premature babies may meet milestones a little later than full-term babies. Take this with you and talk with your child's doctor at every well-child visit about the milestones your child has reached and what to expect next.

Social/Emotional

☐ Is shy or nervous with strangers
☐ Cries when Mom or Dad leaves
☐ Has favorite things and people
☐ Shows fear in some situations
☐ Hands you a book when he wants to hear a story
☐ Repeats sounds or actions to get attention
☐ Puts out arm or leg to help with dressing
☐ Plays games such as "peek-a-boo" and "pat-a-cake"

Language/Communication

☐ Responds to simple spoken requests
☐ Uses simple gestures like shaking head "no" or waving "bye-bye"
☐ Makes sounds with changes in tone (sounds more like speech)
☐ Says "mama" and "dada" and exclamations like "uh-oh!"
☐ Tries to say words you say

Cognitive (learning, thinking, problem-solving)

☐ Explores things in different ways, like shaking, banging, throwing
☐ Finds hidden things easily
☐ Looks at the right picture or thing when it's named
☐ Copies gestures
☐ Starts to use things correctly; for example, drinks from a cup, brushes hair
☐ Bangs two things together
☐ Puts things in a container, takes things out of a container
☐ Lets things go without help
☐ Pokes with index (pointer) finger
☐ Follows simple directions like "pick up the toy"

Movement/Physical Development

☐ Gets to a sitting position without help
☐ Pulls up to stand, walks holding on to furniture ("cruising")
☐ May take a few steps without holding on
☐ May stand alone

Act Early by Talking to Your Child's Doctor If Your Child:

☐ Doesn't crawl
☐ Can't stand when supported
☐ Doesn't search for things that she sees you hide
☐ Doesn't say single words like "mama" or "dada"
☐ Doesn't learn gestures like waving or shaking head
☐ Doesn't point to things
☐ Loses skills she once had

Tell your child's doctor or nurse if you notice any of these signs of possible developmental delay for this age, and talk with someone in your community who is familiar with services for young children in your area, such as your state's public early intervention program.

For more information, go to **www.cdc.gov/concerned** or call **1-800-CDC-INFO.**

*This CDC milestone checklist is not a substitute for a standardized, validated developmental screening tool.

Teaching Your One-Year-Old

Give your child lots of hugs, kisses, and praise for good behavior.

Talk to your child about what you're doing.

For example, *"Now we are getting dressed and Mommy is putting on your shirt."*

Or *"Mommy is washing your hands with a washcloth."*

This is the best way for him to learn language and help his brain make important connections.

Read with your child every day. Aim for at least 20 minutes. Have your child turn the pages. Take turns naming pictures with your child.

Build on what your child says or tries to say, or what he points to. If he points to a truck and says "t" or "truck," say, *"Yes, that's a big, blue truck."*

Give your child crayons and paper and let him draw freely. Show him how to draw lines up and down and across the page. Praise him when he tries to copy them.

Play with blocks, shape sorters, and other toys that encourage your child to use his hands.

Hide small toys and other things and have your child find them.

Count your baby's fingers and toes, touching each one as you count out loud. Encourage them to count with you, but don't worry if they get the numbers wrong. That's not important yet. Just like you are giving them new words, numbers are a part of life. Using them to count fingers and toes helps them understand the concept of numbers.

Give your child pots and pans, rattles, spoons, or small musical instruments like a drum or cymbals. Put on some music and encourage your child to make noise.

Spread baby rice cereal on a cookie sheet and show your child how to use a finger to "write" in the crumbs.

Talk or make silly sounds to your baby through an empty paper towel tube and see how he responds to the change in your normal speaking voice. Let him take a turn and see what sounds he can make.

Encourage your child to explore his toys in new ways; touching, banging, stacking, shaking, and more.

Use tub toys for water play at bath time.

Give your child push toys like a wagon or "kiddie push car."

Send your child on different "errands" around the house, asking him to get his shoes, bring you the ball, or find and deliver his cup. Besides letting him practice his language skills by following directions, this also lets him show you how much he can accomplish by himself, which builds self-confidence. Add silly directions like "Put the cup on your head" to encourage a sense of humor.

Provide lots of safe places for your toddler to explore. But be sure to toddler-proof your home. Lock away medicines and products for cleaning, laundry, lawn care, and car care. Use a safety gate, and lock doors to the outside and basement.

Remember that the first year of your baby's life is a crucial time when important connections are being formed in the brain. Researchers at Cambridge University have discovered that when the brain waves of mothers and babies are out of sync, the babies learn less well. But when the two sets of brain waves are in tune, babies seem to learn more effectively. Babies learn well when their mothers speak to them in a soothing, singsong voice because it holds their attention longer than adult speech. Nursery rhymes are a particularly good way for mothers to get in sync with their babies. Say nursery rhymes and sing songs with actions like "The Itsy Bitsy Spider" and "Wheels on the Bus" daily. Here are a few to get you started. You can find many more online.

Hickory Dickory Dock
Hickory dickory dock,
The mouse ran up the clock.
The clock struck one;
The mouse ran down,
Hickory dickory dock.

Humpty Dumpty
Humpty Dumpty sat on a wall,
Humpty Dumpty had a great fall;
All the king's horses, and all the king's men
Couldn't put Humpty together again.

Pat-A-Cake
Pat-a-cake, pat-a-cake, baker's man!
Bake me a cake as fast as you can.
Pat it, and prick it, and mark it with a "B"
And put it in the oven for baby and me.

Rock-a-Bye Baby
Rock-a-bye baby, on the treetops
When the wind blows, the cradle will rock,
If the bough breaks, the cradle will fall
But mama will catch you, cradle and all.

Twinkle, Twinkle Little Star
Twinkle, twinkle little star, how I wonder what you are.
Up above the world so high, like a diamond in the sky.
Twinkle, twinkle little star, how I wonder what you are.

Itsy Bitsy Spider
The itsy bitsy spider crawled up the water spout.
Down came the rain and washed the spider out.
Out came the sun and dried up all the rain,
and the itsy bitsy spider went up the spout again.

Mary Had a Little Lamb
Mary had a little lamb, whose fleece was white as snow.
And everywhere that Mary went, the lamb was sure to go.
It followed her to school one day, which was against the rules.
It made the children laugh and play to see a lamb at school.
And so the teacher turned it out, but still it lingered near,
and waited patiently about till Mary did appear.
"Why does the lamb love Mary so?" the eager children cry,
"Why Mary loves the lamb, you know." the teacher did reply.

CHAPTER 2

12 TO 24 MONTHS

12 to 15 Months

This is a really fun time for parents, as one-year-olds are able to explore the world in new ways and are eager to do things *all by myself!* They watch their loved ones very carefully and copy a lot of what they say. This is one of the most important ways toddlers learn how the world works.

How do you see your child learning from watching you?

What Your Toddler Can Do	What You Can Do
I'm moving! * I may walk on my own or by holding your hand. * I am learning to crawl upstairs but can't come down yet. * I can throw a ball and turn pages in books.	**Give your child just enough help to reach his goal.** If he wants to stand up, let him hold your fingers for balance. **Support your child as he practices new skills** like climbing stairs. Children need time to work on these new skills…safely! **Encourage your child to turn the pages** when you read together.
I'm starting to talk and understand so much more. * I may use some words like *duh duh* for *dog*. * I can show you what I want through my actions. * I may bang my high chair when I want more food. * If you ask me to, I can point to a body part or a picture in a book.	**Choose books about things that interest your child** like animals or other children. **Build your child's vocabulary.** If she points to or says bus, you can say: *The school bus is driving down the street.* **Name the people, places, and things that your child sees each day:** *That's a garbage truck taking our trash away.* **Play games that involve following directions:** *Throw the ball to me.*
I want to do more for myself. * I say *no* or show you in other ways that I want to do things on my own.	**Involve your child in self-help tasks** like washing his hands. **Follow your child's lead.** Let him choose what toys or games to play.
I love to imitate. * I copy actions I've seen other people do, like stir a pot or talk on the phone.	**Join in your child's play.** If you see her putting a blanket on her toy bear, ask: *Does Teddy need a bottle before bed?* **Give her objects to play with that she sees in "real life,"** like plastic dishes, a toy phone, or a small dust broom.

Temperament

Every child is born with his own individual way of approaching the world. This is called his temperament. For example, some children are easygoing about changes. Others react very strongly to what seems like a small change, like new pajamas. Some children are very active. They love to move. Other children prefer to sit and watch the world around them. Some children enjoy new experiences and meeting new people. Others are slower to warm up in new situations. These are all examples of different temperaments. **There is no right or wrong, better or worse temperament. Temperament is not something your child chooses, and it is not something that you created.** *It's very important for children to be accepted for who they are.* Use what you know about your child's temperament to encourage his strengths and to support him when needed. For example, if your child has a hard time with separations, you can guess that bedtime might be challenging. You can help your child by using the same bedtime routine each night (story, milk, toothbrushing, and lullaby). Your temperament matters too. You might love to meet new people and try new things, but your child doesn't. Being aware of this difference is important. It helps you understand how your child's needs may be different from yours. It also helps you learn what to do in order to support and respect your child for who she is.

Picky Eaters

Picky eating is very common at this age. Most children are feeding themselves. This means they are able to choose what to eat—or not eat. The key is to avoid turning mealtime into a power struggle. Offer your child three or four healthy food choices that she usually likes at each meal time (like pieces of turkey and cheese, cooked peas, and some banana). Then let her decide what and how much she wants to eat. Remember, as long as your child seems to enjoy eating and has the energy to play and interact with you, she is probably doing just fine. Be sure to talk to your child's healthcare provider if you are concerned or have questions.

Sharing

The majority of parents (51%) believe that 15-month-olds are able to share. Actually most children learn to share and take turns **between the ages of two and three.** Even after that, they need a lot of practice and help with these important social skills. Young toddlers can seem like "big kids" in many ways, but **at 15 months toddlers do not yet have the self-control necessary to share and take turns.** They can't stop themselves from reaching for a favorite toy, even while someone else is playing with it. This is because the part of their brain responsible for self-control is still developing. But you can begin teaching your child about sharing. Explain the rule: *"We are going to take turns with the Jack-in-the-Box. Derek is going to use it now."* Then help your child focus on another activity while his friend has a turn. Most importantly, stay calm and be patient. Sharing is a skill that comes with time, and with your support and guidance.[8]

---

8   www.zerotothree.org reprinted with permission.

15-Month-Old Milestones

How your child plays, learns, speaks, acts, and moves offers important clues about his or her development. Check the milestones your child has reached by 15 months. As you use this resource, remember that your child may develop skills faster or slower than indicated here and still be growing just fine. Premature babies may meet milestones a little later than full-term babies. Take this with you and talk with your child's doctor at every well-child visit about the milestones your child has reached and what to expect next.

Walking

Your child is probably taking at least a few steps on her own. About half of 15-month-olds can walk well. A few are even running.

Speech

Most 15-month-olds say at least one word. Half can say at least two words. And some tots will have now ventured past "dada" and "mama" to form a growing vocabulary that includes words like "dog" or "juice."

Teething

First molars may be starting to erupt. For some children, cutting teeth can be painful and bothersome. For others, you just happen to notice one day a new pearly white poking through the gums.

Identification

Your child is starting to understand what everyday objects are used for—a broom is for sweeping and a wooden spoon is for stirring. Some 15-month-olds can identify and point to a few body parts when you ask them to show you.

*This milestone checklist is not a substitute for a standardized, validated developmental screening tool.

12 TO 24 MONTHS

Behavior

How To Discipline A 15-Month-Old

While it's great to have an active and (mostly) happy toddler, they have their challenging behaviors such as tantrums, separation anxiety, and throwing things. It might seem like your child is "misbehaving" at times, but at 15 months, he probably doesn't realize he's acting up. He simply wants to see what it's like to color on the wall or to explore the couch by climbing it. Throwing things or hitting gets him attention and, sometimes, exactly what he wants. To start to teach your child good behavior, you'll want to set up some boundaries and consequences.

Here are a few tips that may work in disciplining your 15-month-old:

Hide things that are off-limits. You won't have to keep telling your child "no" when she touches the remote, a Magic Marker, or Daddy's phone if they are out of her line of sight and reach.

Set clear rules and consequences. And stick to them! If your child sees that pulling the dog's tail gets him a time-out every time, he'll—eventually—stop it.

Distract and redirect. Dwelling on negative behavior won't really teach any lessons at this age. If your child acts out, remove her from the situation and distract her with a positive activity.

Respond to wanted behaviors more than you punish unwanted behaviors (use only very brief time-outs). Always tell or show your child what she should do instead.

Stay calm. It's natural to want to freak out when your child does, but try to demonstrate calm behavior. Over time, he'll start to learn how to act from you.

Teaching Your Toddler:

Read to your toddler daily.

Ask her to find objects for you or name body parts and objects.

Play matching games with your toddler, like shape sorting and simple puzzles.

Encourage him to explore and try new things.

Help to develop your toddler's language by talking with her and adding to words she starts. For example, if your toddler says "baba," you can respond, "Yes, you are right—that is a bottle."

Encourage your child's growing independence by letting him help with dressing himself and feeding himself.

Encourage your toddler's curiosity and ability to recognize common objects by taking field trips together to the park or going on a bus ride.

Healthy Bodies

Give your child water and plain milk instead of sugary drinks. After the first year, when your nursing toddler is eating more and different solid foods, breast milk is still an ideal addition to his diet.

Your toddler might become a very picky and erratic eater. Toddlers need less food because they don't grow as fast. It's best not to battle with him over this. Offer a selection of healthy foods and let him choose what he wants. Keep trying new foods; it might take time for him to learn to like them.

Limit screen time. For children younger than two years of age, the AAP recommends that it's **best if toddlers not watch any screen media. Studies show that it interferes with normal brain development. UC Irvine researchers have found that fragmented and chaotic maternal care can disrupt proper brain development in infants, which can lead to emotional disorders later in life. Be sure you are looking at your baby more than your cell phone.**

Your toddler will seem to be moving continually—running, kicking, climbing, or jumping. Let him be active—he's developing his coordination and becoming strong.

Child Safety First

Because your child is moving around more, he will come across more dangers as well. Dangerous situations can happen quickly, so keep a close eye on your child. Here are a few tips to help keep your growing toddler safe:

Do NOT leave your toddler near or around water (for example, bathtubs, pools, ponds, lakes, whirlpools, or the ocean) without someone watching her. Fence off backyard pools. Drowning is the leading cause of injury and death among this age group.

Block off stairs with a small gate or fence. Lock doors to dangerous places such as the garage or basement.

Ensure that your home is toddler-proof by placing plug covers on all unused electrical outlets.

Keep kitchen appliances, irons, and heaters out of reach of your toddler. Turn pot handles toward the back of the stove.

Keep sharp objects such as scissors, knives, and pens in a safe place.

Lock up medicines, household cleaners, and poisons.

Do NOT leave your toddler alone in any vehicle (that means a car, truck, or van) even for a few moments.

Store any guns in a safe place out of his reach.

Keep your child's car seat rear-facing as long as possible. According to the National Highway Traffic Safety Administration, it's the best way to keep her safe. Your child should remain in a rear-facing car seat until she reaches the top height or weight limit allowed by the car seat's manufacturer. Once your child outgrows the rear-facing car seat, she is ready to travel in a forward-facing car seat with a harness.

15 to 18 Months

Your toddler is using all his new physical, thinking, and language skills to be a good problem solver. He might push a stool to the counter and try to climb up as he points to the cookie jar and says something like *Mine*!

How do you see your toddler figuring things out?

What Your Toddler Can Do	What You Can Do
I'm using my body to explore and learn. * I am walking and may be running and climbing. * I can scribble with a crayon and build a block tower. * I can feed myself.	**Encourage your child to use his fingers and hands to explore.** Let him scribble, tap a toy piano, or hold a bubble wand. **Play "baby Olympics."** Create some safe challenges—like climbing over a stack of pillows—for your child to master.
I'm using language to understand the world around me. * I can understand simple questions and directions like, *Kick the ball to me*. * I communicate by combining sounds and actions—pointing to a cup and saying *wawa* for water. * By 18 months, I may say as many as 20 words.	**Ask your child questions.** *Would you like yogurt or a banana for a snack?* **Put her gestures into words.** *You're pointing at the bird flying in the sky.* **Read, sing together, and make up rhymes and stories.** This builds a love of language and words.
I am beginning to understand my feelings and other's feelings too. * I may try to comfort someone who seems sad. * I repeat sounds and actions that make someone laugh. * My feelings can be hard for me to handle. I may start having tantrums and will need your help to calm down.	**Read books that talk about feelings.** Connect what you are reading to your child's experiences: *That little boy in the book felt sad saying goodbye to his daddy, just like you do sometimes.* **Stay calm during tantrums.** Take deep breaths, count to ten, or whatever helps you to not react. Staying calm helps your child recover more quickly.
I'm becoming a good problem solver. * I may do something over and over to figure out how it works. * I use objects the way they are supposed to be used—like talking on a toy telephone. * I imitate what I see others do—like trying to wipe the table with a sponge.	**Let your child repeat the same activity, if he wants to.** It may be boring to you but is important practice for him. **Once your child has learned a new skill, like throwing the ball, add a twist:** Set up a laundry basket for him to toss the ball into.

Problem Solving

The ability to solve problems is very important for being successful in school and in life. When you see your toddler getting into everything, think of it as his way of problem-solving—figuring out how things work. Toddlers problem-solve by using their bodies and their minds to make a plan to reach their goals. For example, toddlers are solving a problem when they tip over their sippy cup to see how to make the liquid come out. Toddlers are also solving problems by using their past experiences to help them understand new situations. For example, your child may begin throwing everything into the trash—garbage or not. He is remembering that throwing his napkin out after lunch makes you happy. He just hasn't learned yet what *not* to toss out! Children also learn how to solve problems by imitating what the people who care for them do. So when they see adults staying calm and not giving up when they face a challenge, children learn to keep trying too.

Independence

Your 16-month-old may want to do everything by himself, but sometimes that just isn't possible. Here's how you can help:

- **Be creative.** If he wants to feed himself but can't yet use a spoon, give him one spoon to hold while you feed him with the other.

- **Find an alternative.** Explain: *These sharp knives are for Mommy and Daddy to use.* Then show her how to use her hands or a blunt plastic knife to cut her food.

- **Be his coach.** Offer just enough support so that he can achieve the goal himself. You might put your hand over his to help him zip his jacket.

- **Let your child safely practice new skills.** She can practice pouring water out in the backyard or by using a small plastic pitcher in the bathtub.

- **Support your child in reaching her goal.** If her block tower keeps falling, suggest she add some more blocks on the bottom for support.

- **Do chores together.** Pushing a broom, for example, helps children solve problems like how to get the crumbs into the dustpan.

- **Teach your child to ask for help.** When you see him getting frustrated as he tries to solve a problem, you might say: *It can be hard to get that Jack-in-the-Box to pop up! Would you like some help? Let's try turning this knob together.*

Self-awareness

At 18 months children begin developing a sense of self-awareness—the knowledge that they are individuals with their own feelings, thoughts, likes, and dislikes. Next they realize that other people have their own feelings, thoughts and preferences too. This helps children learn empathy.

They can imagine how another person feels.

To help your child develop empathy:

- **Talk about other's feelings.** *Kayla is feeling sad because you took her toy car. Let's give Kayla back her car and then choose another one for you.*

- **Suggest how children can show empathy.** *Let's get Jason some ice for his boo-boo.*

- **Empathize with your child.** *Are you feeling scared of that dog? He is a nice dog but he is barking really loud. That can be scary. I will hold you until he walks by.*[9]

---

[9] www.zerotothree.org reprinted with permission.

18-Month Milestones

How your child plays, learns, speaks, acts, and moves offers important clues about his or her development. Check the milestones your child has reached by 18 months. As you use this resource, remember that your child may develop skills faster or slower than indicated here and still be growing just fine. Premature babies may meet milestones a little later than full-term babies. Take this with you and talk with your child's doctor at every well-child visit about the milestones your child has reached and what to expect next.

Social/Emotional

- ☐ Likes to hand things to others as play
- ☐ May have temper tantrums
- ☐ May be afraid of strangers
- ☐ Shows affection to familiar people
- ☐ Plays simple pretend, such as feeding a doll
- ☐ May cling to caregivers in new situations
- ☐ Points to show others something interesting
- ☐ Explores alone but with parent close by

Language/Communication

- ☐ Says several single words
- ☐ Says and shakes head "no"
- ☐ Points to show someone what he wants

Cognitive (learning, thinking, problem-solving)

- ☐ Knows what ordinary things are for; for example, telephone, brush, spoon
- ☐ Points to get the attention of others
- ☐ Shows interest in a doll or stuffed animal by pretending to feed it
- ☐ Points to one body part
- ☐ Scribbles on his own
- ☐ Can follow one-step verbal commands without any gestures, for example, sits when you say "sit down"

Movement/Physical Development

☐ Walks alone
☐ May walk up steps and run
☐ Pulls toys while walking
☐ Can help undress herself
☐ Drinks from a cup
☐ Eats with a spoon

Act Early by Talking to Your Child's Doctor if Your Child:

☐ Doesn't point to show things to others
☐ Can't walk
☐ Doesn't know what familiar things are for
☐ Doesn't copy others
☐ Doesn't gain new words
☐ Doesn't have at least 6 words
☐ Doesn't notice or mind when a caregiver leaves or returns
☐ Loses skills he once had

Tell your child's doctor or nurse if you notice any of these signs of possible developmental delay for this age, and talk with someone in your community who is familiar with services for young children in your area, such as your state's public early intervention program. For more information, go to **www.cdc.gov/concerned** or call **1-800-CDC-INFO**.

The American Academy of Pediatrics recommends that children be screened for general development and autism at the 18-month visit. Ask your child's doctor about your child's developmental screening.

*This CDC milestone checklist is not a substitute for a standardized, validated developmental screening tool.

18 to 24 Months

This is a delightful stage as children begin to talk and talk and then talk some more. Toddlers are also starting to pretend. This is a big step in their development and makes life really fun and often very funny.

How do you see your child starting to use her imagination?

What Your Toddler Can Do	What You Can Do
I am learning new words every day. * I may say as many as 50 to 100 words by my second birthday. * I may even put two words together to make my first sentences!	**Turn your child's words and phrases into sentences.** When he says, *More milk,* you can say: *You want more milk in your cup?* **Talk as you read.** Ask your child questions about the pictures and stories you read together.
I need help to begin learning self-control. * I understand *no,* but I still can't control my feelings and actions. * I may get frustrated when I can't do something by myself. Please be patient with me!	**Put your child's feelings into words.** *I know you're really mad that I turned the TV off. It's okay to feel mad. Instead of TV, would you like to read or play with blocks now?*
I am beginning to use my imagination. * I may feed my doll pretend food. * I might make *brrrmm* noises when I play with cars.	**Play pretend with your toddler.** You can be a puppy, barking and running after a ball. **Jump-start your child's imagination** with dress-up clothes, animal figures, blocks, and plastic food and dishes.
I am a little scientist always testing things out! * I love to fill and dump and open and close things to see how they work. * I may start to sort objects. I might put all my trains in one place and all my cars in another.	**Help your child practice sorting.** Ask your child to help you sort the laundry by putting socks in one pile and shirts in another. **Encourage lots of exploration.** Fill and dump with water or sand. Make an indoor "sandbox" of dry oatmeal or fall leaves.
I am becoming an even better problem solver. * I may blow on my food when you tell me dinner is hot or try to get my own jacket on, without any help.	**Help your child solve a problem but don't do it all for him.** The more he does, the more he learns. **Play games that use problem-solving skills.** Try three- or four-piece puzzles or building with blocks.

Language Development

Learning to talk is one of the most important milestones of the first few years. How and when young children learn to use spoken words is different for every child. Some children may use words early and often, but others may take longer to speak. If you have questions about your child's language development, talk with your healthcare provider or other trusted professional.

Build your child's vocabulary through repetition. When your child uses the same sound over and over to name an object, it is considered a "word." If your child always says *muh* when he wants milk, it means that he understands this sound stands for a specific object—that yummy white stuff. Correct pronunciation will come over time. You can help him learn how to pronounce words by saying what you know he means: *Do you want more milk?*

Notice how your child uses his actions to communicate. Nonverbal communication is very important. When a toddler takes your hand and leads you to a toy, she is using her action to say, *I want to play with this toy.* If your child is communicating through actions like this, her spoken language skills will likely follow. You can help by repeating the message your child is sending: *You'd like me to play with you. Here I come!*

Talk together with your child. The more you talk with your child, the more words he will learn. **He's learning language from you—his first, and best, teacher.**

Understanding No

Toddlers understand a lot of what you tell them. They just don't have much self-control yet. So while your son may stop when he hears you say *no*, he cannot stop himself from doing it again. He can't tell himself: *I really want to play with this lamp, but it's against the rules so I better not.* For now, make your home as child-safe as possible so you can use fewer *no's*. When you do set a limit (*No touching the lamp*), guide your child away from it and offer a substitute—like a flashlight—to play with. **Self-control takes years to develop. Your child will need lots of patience and consistency from you along the way.**

Parents may deal with challenging behavior in their toddlers every three to nine minutes. Testing is part of a toddler's healthy development. They do this by trying out different behaviors and seeing what reactions they get. ***How you respond makes a big difference in what your child learns and how she behaves.***

When you set limits:

Be clear about rules. Toddlers need lots of reminders about rules because their memory is still developing.

Be specific. Say, *Please put the blocks in the box* instead of *Clean up your toys.*

Be consistent. Use the same consequences. For example, every time your child throws a toy off the high chair, take the toy away for a few minutes. Then let him try again.

Stay calm. All children test the rules. The more calmly you respond, the more effective you will be at teaching your child.[10]

---

10 www.zerotothree.org reprinted with permission.

Teaching Your 18-Month-Old

Provide a safe, loving environment. <u>It's important to be consistent and predictable.</u>

Every day let your child know you love her by a touch, word, or gesture.

Read books daily for at least 20 minutes and talk about the pictures using simple words. **Remember that this is a crucial time for brain development, and reading is the best thing you can do to help make your baby smarter!** Go to the library and ask the librarian for age-appropriate books.

Talk to your child every day and describe what is happening.

For example, *"Look out the window—it's raining today! You will have to wear your yellow raincoat and boots to stay dry. Can you help me find the umbrella?"*

Praise good behaviors more than you punish bad behaviors (use only very brief time-outs).

Comment often on what your child does well.

Describe her emotions. For example, say, "You are happy when we read this book."

Encourage empathy. For example, when he sees a friend or family member who is sad, encourage him to hug or pat the other child or family member.

Encourage pretend play. Dress up using hats, shoes, jewelry, and other props.

Make sure your child has plenty of chances to run, jump, and play outside. Take him to a playground or park every week.

Copy your child's words.

Use words that describe feelings and emotions. Use simple, clear phrases.

Ask simple questions.

Hide things under blankets and pillows and encourage him to find them.

Play with blocks, balls, puzzles, books, and toys that teach cause and effect and problem-solving.

Name pictures in books and body parts.

Provide toys that encourage pretend play; for example, dolls, play telephones.

Provide toys that she can push or pull safely.

Provide balls for her to kick, roll, and throw.

Encourage him to drink from his cup and use a spoon, no matter how messy.

Blow bubbles and let your child pop them.

Rice is a fun sensory play item. It's cheap and kids love the texture falling through their fingers. Use cups of different sizes for them to explore pouring and scooping the rice.

Let your child explore playing with wet spaghetti.

Create a fort out of a cardboard box, play tunnel, or playhouse. Include an entrance and an exit, and encourage your child to go in and out. (You might need to show him how at first.) Make it even more fun with some pretend play, like knocking on the door and asking if anyone is at home.

Repeat nursery rhymes, lullabies, and simple songs daily. Repetition, rhythm, and rhyme are all elements that help your baby learn language.

Play a game at bath time. Using plastic toys, show your child how some objects **float**, and some **sink**. *Which toy do you think will sink?*

Make a Soapy Sensory Jar using an empty peanut butter or jelly jar with a lid. Fill the jar halfway with water. Add food coloring of your choice, dish soap and glitter. Screw the lid on tight and shake. Your child will love seeing how the liquid, glitter, bubbles and colors swirl and move about. Sit on the floor and roll the jar back and forth to each other.

Two-Year-Old Milestones

How your child plays, learns, speaks, acts, and moves offers important clues about his or her development. Check the milestones your child has reached by their second birthday. As you use this resource, remember that your child may develop skills faster or slower than indicated here and still be growing just fine. Premature babies may meet milestones a little later than full-term babies. Take this with you and talk with your child's doctor at every well-child visit about the milestones your child has reached and what to expect next.

Social and Emotional

- ☐ Copies others, especially adults and older children
- ☐ Shows more and more independence
- ☐ Shows defiant behavior (doing what he has been told not to)
- ☐ Plays mainly beside other children, but is beginning to include other children, such as in chase games

Language/Communication

- ☐ Points to things or pictures when they are named
- ☐ Knows names of familiar people and body parts
- ☐ Says sentences with 2 to 4 words
- ☐ Follows simple instructions
- ☐ Repeats words overheard in conversation
- ☐ Points to things in a book

Cognitive (learning, thinking, problem-solving)

- ☐ Finds things even when hidden under two or three covers
- ☐ Begins to sort shapes and colors
- ☐ Completes sentences and rhymes in familiar books
- ☐ Plays simple make-believe games
- ☐ Builds towers of 4 or more blocks
- ☐ Might use one hand more than the other
- ☐ Follows two-step instructions such as *"Pick up your shoes and put them in the closet."*
- ☐ Names items in a picture book, such as a cat, bird, or dog

Movement/Physical Development

☐ Stands on tiptoe
☐ Kicks a ball
☐ Begins to run
☐ Climbs onto and down from furniture without help
☐ Walks up and down stairs holding on
☐ Throws ball overhand
☐ Makes or copies straight lines and circles

Act early by talking to your child's doctor if your child:

☐ Doesn't use 2-word phrases (for example, "drink milk")
☐ Doesn't know what to do with common things, like a brush, phone, fork, spoon
☐ Doesn't copy actions and words
☐ Doesn't follow simple instructions
☐ Doesn't walk steadily
☐ Loses skills she once had

If you are concerned, ACT EARLY! Tell your child's doctor or nurse if you notice any of these signs of possible developmental delay for this age.

The American Academy of Pediatrics recommends that children be screened for general development using standardized, validated tools at 9, 18, and 24 or 30 months, and for autism at 18 and 24 months, or whenever a parent or provider has a concern. Ask your child's doctor about your child's developmental screening.

*This CDC milestone checklist is not a substitute for a standardized, validated developmental screening tool.

Notes:

CHAPTER 3

24 TO 36 MONTHS

24 to 30 Months

This is an exciting time as older toddlers are using their growing language skills to tell you what they are thinking and feeling. They are also building friendships with other children. And their growing physical skills—walking, running, and climbing—help them explore the world in more adventurous ways.

What do you find most amazing about your child's development at this stage?

What Your Toddler Can Do	What You Can Do
I use my body to get me places. * I can walk upstairs one foot at a time. * I can walk backward. * I can balance on one foot, which helps me climb.	**Go on a neighborhood walk.** Let your child stop to check out what is interesting to her. **Play "island hop."** Line up pieces of paper on the floor and help your child jump from one to the next.
I am using language to tell you what I'm feeling and thinking. * I can make longer sentences: *Mama play truck?* * My favorite words may be *no*, *me*, and *mine*. * I may get overwhelmed by my strong feelings and have trouble putting them into words. * I might need your help to calm down.	**Ask about your child's ideas:** *What part of the book did you like?* **Acknowledge feelings and teach social skills at the same time:** *I know the doll stroller is your favorite toy, but Thomas would like a turn pushing it.* **Help your child recover from a tantrum.** Some children respond to being comforted. Others do better with some alone time in a safe, quiet place.
I am getting really good at playing pretend. * I can use one object to stand in for another. A shoebox may become a bed for my stuffed hippo. * I laugh at silly things, like the idea that my toy car might go *moo* instead of *beep beep*. * Sometimes I get scared. I am getting so good at using my imagination but am not always sure what's real and what's pretend.	**Use pretend play to help your child handle challenging situations.** You might act out a story together about meeting a new babysitter. **Let your child lead the play.** Ask: *Who should I be? What will happen next?* **Respond sensitively to your child's fears.** Explain what is real and pretend. This builds trust and security.
I want to make friends but still need help with sharing. * I like watching other children and may copy what I see them do. * I may have one or two good friends.	**Give your child regular chances to play with children her age.** This builds social skills. **Help your child with conflicts around sharing and turn taking.** Let her know you understand that sharing is hard. Help her find another toy to play with until it's her turn. Use a kitchen timer to help her learn to wait.

Toilet Training

When and how you help your child learn to use the potty depends on how ready your child is. Your culture—your family's beliefs and values about toilet training—also matters. There is not one "right" way to toilet train your child. Most children develop control over their bowels and bladder by 18 months. This is necessary for children to physically be able to use the toilet. How emotionally ready a child is to use the potty depends on the individual child. Starting to train your child earlier does not necessarily mean she will learn to use the potty sooner. One study showed that children whose parents started training them before 27 months took longer to learn to use the potty compared to children whose parents started after 27 months. Finding a toilet-training method that works for your family is the key. No matter how you do it, remember that potty training takes time, with many accidents along the way. **Never punish your child for having an accident.** Children with special needs may take longer to learn to use the potty. They may also need special equipment and a lot of help and patience from you. For questions about toilet training, talk with your healthcare provider or early intervention specialist.

Parents and children each have their own jobs to do when it comes to potty training. Parents are responsible for creating a supportive learning environment.

Parents should:

Respect that your child is in control of her body.

Ask your child whether she wants to use the potty or wear a diaper/pull-up each day.

Teach your child words for body parts, urine, and bowel movements.

Offer your child the tools such as a small potty, potty seat, or stool necessary to succeed at toileting. **Handle potty accidents without anger.**

Avoid punishment as well as too much praise around the toilet use.

Your child:

Decides whether to use the toilet or a diaper/pull-up.

Learns his body's signals for urine and bowel movements.

Uses the toilet at his own speed.[11]

---

[11] Signs That Children Are Ready for Potty Training: Children's Hospital Boston, Woolf, A., Kenna, M., & Shane, H., Eds. Children's Hospital Guide to Your Child's Health and Development. Cambridge, MA: Perseus Books, 2001. Toilet learning: Anticipatory guidance with a child-oriented approach. Pediatrics & Child Health, 5(6), 333-335.

Positive Parenting Behavior Tips:

Tantrums

Tantrums are common among toddlers. They happen when children have lost their ability to handle a difficult situation, such as having something they want denied. **This mood swing is normal because at this stage, your child is learning about his world by trying out everything.** And when he oversteps his limits and is pulled back, he will often react with a tantrum in the form of crying, hitting, or screaming. Try not to overreact by scolding or punishing him too much. Explain calmly why he can't misbehave, and then try to distract him with a better choice.

For example, if you are having trouble getting him dressed and out the door in the morning, offer him choices.

"Do you want to wear the red shirt or the blue one?"

"Do you want to drink from the green cup or the yellow one?"

Help your child manage frustration by:

Acknowledging his feelings. *I know you are mad that you can't have more ice cream. It's okay to feel mad. When you calm down, we can figure out what to do next.*

Offering choices. *Would you like an apple or a banana?*

Using humor. *"Mr. Apple wants you to eat him. Oh no, now Miss Banana is pushing Apple out of the way so you will choose her instead!"* Humor cuts the tension and helps children calm down.

Helping your child learn appropriate behaviors is one of the toughest jobs of parenting. Children feel secure in a home where they know they are loved by parents who are in charge.

You can help him develop positive feelings by encouraging him to behave. Here are some suggestions:

- **Set reasonable limits** that allow him to play and explore without any danger. Children are very curious at this age and need to be able to explore their environment in order to learn and grow. **Remember that 80% of their brain is formed by the time they are three years old!**

- **Praise him every day**; when he plays wells with others, feeds, dresses or undresses without your help, or when you start an activity together and he finishes it without your help. As you do, he'll start to feel good about himself and want to please you more. For most children, this simple step helps negative behavior begin to fade away.

- **When correcting behavior, try to remain calm, firm, and positive**. Don't correct him constantly without kindness. Use the positive approach. Tell your child what you want him to do. For example, say, *"Sit down in the chair"* rather than *"Don't stand on the chair."* When he does as you asked, praise him for it.

- **Avoid long explanations he won't understand**. Keep it short and simple: *"We don't hit other people. That hurts. No hitting!"*

- **Be consistent in your discipline**. Children want and need limits. They feel safe when they understand the rules and know where the boundaries are and what to expect.

- **Make sure your child is getting plenty of good, positive attention from you**. Many times children misbehave just to get your attention. **Make sure you look at your child more often than your cell phone.**

- **Don't forget humor.** Children love it! If you can distract bad behavior with humor or silliness, your child will be happier and better behaved.

- **No matter how frustrated you get, try to remain positive**. Children at this age respond well to praise, so praise him every time he is behaving well or doing what you asked.[12]

---

[12] www.zerotothree.org reprinted with permission.

30-Month-Old Milestones

Doctors use certain milestones to tell if a toddler is developing as expected. There's a wide range of what's considered normal, so as you use this resource, remember that your child may develop skills faster or slower than indicated here and still be growing just fine. Premature babies may meet milestones a little later than full-term babies. Take this list with you and talk with your child's doctor at every well-child visit about the milestones your child has reached and what to expect next.

Communication and Language Skills

- ☐ Says short phrases of 3-4 words
- ☐ Vocabulary of 100-250 words
- ☐ Is understandable to others 50% of the time
- ☐ Speaks using pronouns (I, me, you)
- ☐ Asks many "What?" and "Where?" questions

Movement and Physical Development

- ☐ Teething
- ☐ Washes and dries hands
- ☐ Brushes teeth with help
- ☐ Pulls pants up with assistance
- ☐ Jumps in place
- ☐ Kicks a ball
- ☐ Throws a ball overhand
- ☐ Walks up and down stairs
- ☐ Builds a tower of blocks

Social and Emotional Development

- ☐ Enjoys pretend play
- ☐ Starts to play with, not just alongside, other kids
- ☐ Can tell you when he or she needs a diaper change or has to go to the potty
- ☐ Refers to himself or herself by name

24 TO 36 MONTHS

Cognitive Skills (Thinking and Learning)

☐ Begins to develop a sense of humor (e.g., thinks silly things, such as a story about a barking cat, are funny)
☐ Understands the concept of one item or thing (e.g., "Give me one block.")

When to Talk to Your Doctor

Every child develops at his or her own pace, but certain signs could indicate a delay in development. Talk to your doctor if your child:

☐ Does not engage in pretend play
☐ Doesn't speak, or makes vowel sounds but no consonants or words
☐ Doesn't recognize simple emotions (happy, sad) in others
☐ Has lost skills he once had
☐ Shows weakness on one side of the body

If you are concerned, act early! Tell your child's doctor or nurse if you notice any of these signs of possible developmental delay for this age.

The American Academy of Pediatrics recommends that children be screened for general development using standardized, validated tools at 9, 18, and 24 or 30 months and for autism at 18 and 24 months or whenever a parent or provider has a concern. Ask your child's doctor about your child's developmental screening.

*This CDC milestone checklist is not a substitute for a standardized, validated developmental screening tool.

30-Month-Old Behavior

Tantrums. At 30 months old, it is common for your child to throw tantrums. However, the peak time frame for tantrums tends to be between 17 and 24 months, so you might notice soon that their frequency is starting to decline. If your child has frequent tantrums (several per day), discuss it with the pediatrician—some kids need extra help learning to calm themselves down.

Independence. Your child can probably undress herself now; some 30-month-olds pull on their own pants and socks too.

Fickleness. He's torn between wanting to be a big kid and wanting to be a baby. So some days, he might do things on his own and others, he insists you do it all. Some parents find that their 30-month-olds are well behaved at school or daycare, but wild at home. He may be anxious or shy around strangers too.

Regression. It's normal for a two-year-old to regress in some ways, such as starting to tantrum more or having more potty accidents. Maybe your child asks for an old blanket, toy, or pacifier. This is often just a normal part of growing up, but tell the doctor about any setbacks that concern you.

Notes:

_____
_____
_____
_____
_____
_____
_____
_____
_____
_____
_____
_____
_____
_____
_____
_____
_____
_____
_____
_____
_____
_____
_____
_____
_____

Teaching Your Two-Year-Old

Remember that 80% of your child's brain is formed by age three!

So read to your child every day. Reading is the single most important thing you can do for your child to succeed in school. Even five minutes a day makes a big difference, but aim for 20 minutes daily. Try to make it part of your bedtime routine. When reading to your child, ask him to point to things in the pictures and repeat words after you.

Every day let your child know you love her by a touch, word, or gesture.

Encourage your child to help with simple chores at home, like sweeping, folding laundry, or making dinner. Praise your child for being a good helper.

Give your child attention and praise when he follows instructions. **Limit attention for bad behavior. Spend a lot more time praising good behaviors than punishing bad ones.**

Be a word giver. Teach your child to identify and say the names of household items, animals, and other common things. Teach your child the names of his body parts, including **elbow**, **wrist**, **knee**, **ankle**, **shoulder**, **stomach**, and **chest**.

Show your child how to brush all his teeth, inside and out, for two minutes. Brush your teeth at the same time. Always do the final brushing yourself to make sure all teeth are clean. **Make sure your child brushes his teeth EVERY DAY.**

Avoid giving your cell phone to your child to keep him entertained or quiet. Interact with him instead. Play a game, sing songs, or talk about what is happening at the moment. **The more you interact with your child, the happier and smarter he will be.**

Mark your child's height on a wall and date it. She will love seeing herself grow. Explain *feet* and *inches*.

Turn everyday routines into playful moments. Make a game of cleaning up. Praise your child whenever he is cooperative.

Hide your child's toys around the room and let him find them. Explore with him, using cues like "warmer" and "colder" to guide him.

Variations: Use flashlights for the search, or hide several objects at one time.

Help your child do puzzles with shapes, colors, or farm animals. Name each piece when your child puts it in place.

Encourage your child to play with blocks. Take turns building towers and knocking them down. Playing with blocks helps your child's brain to make important connections necessary for school success, especially in math. You can use household items like cans, boxes, or books for pretend blocks.

Do art projects with your child using crayons, paint, and paper. Let them draw lines and circles. Describe what your child makes and hang it on the wall or refrigerator.

Ask your child to help you open doors and drawers and turn pages in a book or magazine.

Use pictures of the alphabet, numbers, animals, the solar system, and special sights in nature to create a stimulating environment in your child's room. Follow their interests.

Two-year-olds have fun rolling and stacking cups, and pretending to drink/eat. They also love to play with empty pots and pans or empty food containers.

Play a learning game of concentration. Put three items out and remove one. Have your child identify which object was removed.

Teach your child **positional words** such as **top, bottom, into, outside, around, over, under, upside down, on, beside, corner.** Using games you can tell your child to get *behind* the door, or *under* the table. Using their favorite toy, ask them to put it in the position you name.

Teach your child how to kick a ball and how to throw a ball over head.

Give your child simple two-step directions. *"Pick up your shoes and go put them in your closet."*

At this age, children still play next to (not with) each other and don't share well. For play dates, give children lots of toys to play with. Watch them closely and step in if they fight or argue and gently encourage them to get along and be kind to one another.

When your child gets upset, **stay calm** to help him feel safe and get back in control.

Albert Einstein once said, "Imagination is more important than knowledge."

A rich imagination helps us become more creative and interesting. You can help your child think more creatively and develop his imagination. Children love to play pretend games. Encourage your child to do this and even join in with him. Provide him with plenty of props:

24 TO 36 MONTHS

A blanket thrown over two chairs becomes a fort.

Old clothes help him pretend to be different people.

A large appliance box becomes a house.

Empty cereal boxes and cans are transformed into the grocery store.

Try "cloud watching" with your child on a warm day. Take turns imagining what each cloud shape could be.

Have a tea party with dolls and stuffed animals.

Help your child be a good problem solver by giving her the support she needs without completely solving problems for her. Give your child a chance to do things for herself.

Encourage your child to keep trying.

Ask your child lots of **who, what, when, where, how** questions that get him thinking as he nears age three.

30 to 36 Months

Older toddlers are full of personality and energy. They want to know the reason for everything, which is why you may hear your child ask *why?* a lot!

What kinds of questions are your child asking? What is she curious about?

What Your Toddler Can Do	What You Can Do
My body helps me do "big kid" stuff now! * I can pedal a tricycle. * I can dress myself with your help. * I can draw a line. * I can turn a knob or unscrew a cap.	**Let your child scribble with markers and crayons.** This builds early writing skills. **Give your child plenty of chances to practice more advanced physical skills** like paddling and climbing. **Childproof again** so that your child's new ability to open caps and door knobs doesn't lead to danger.
I use language to express my thoughts and feelings. * By age 3, I may use as many as 900 words. * I understand sentences with two or more ideas (*You can have a snack when we get home*). * I ask questions. * I know my first and last name.	**Introduce new words to build your child's vocabulary:** *Is your snack scrumptious?* **Ask questions that require more than a yes or no answer**: *Where do you think the squirrel is taking his nap?* **Be patient with your child's *Why?* questions.** Ask him what he thinks before you answer.
I am using my new thinking skills to solve problems. * I can remember what happened yesterday. * I act out my own stories. * I'm becoming a "logical thinker." When I am pretending that it is bedtime for Teddy, I'll put a blanket on him and sing him a lullaby.	**At dinner time or before bed, talk with your child about her day.** This builds memory and language skills. **Encourage your child to use logic in everyday situations:** *It's raining. What do we need in order to stay dry?*
My friends are very important to me. * I like playing with other children. * I may have one or two close friends. * I notice how people are the same and different—like their skin color and size.	**Help children deal with the conflicts around sharing and turn taking:** *There is only one train. I will put the timer on and you will each have five minutes to play with it. While you wait for your turn, you can choose to play with cars or another toy.* **Help your child be sensitive to differences among people:** *Yes, people do come in all different sizes.*

24 TO 36 MONTHS

Making Friends

Between 30 and 36 months, toddlers really enjoy playing with friends—doing things like acting out stories, building together with blocks, or exploring the playground. Friendships are great fun. They also help children develop important social skills like taking turns, sharing, and helping others. Through friendships, children learn to communicate with others, resolve disagreements, and understand others' thoughts and feelings. Children who are friendly, confident, and who can cooperate with others are most likely to succeed in a classroom setting. Keep in mind that brothers and sisters are often a child's first friends, even though it may not seem like it some days! Sibling relationships provide daily practice with sharing and cooperating. They also offer children opportunities to show compassion and loving support.

Teaching Your Child:

Make time for play. Encourage brothers, sisters, and cousins to play together. Organize play dates with friends. Join a parenting group or attend community events like library story hours.

Give nonverbal feedback. Give your child an encouraging smile when he is unsure about sharing.

Notice positive behavior. *You two figured out how to share the trains. Nice job!*

Help children understand others' feelings. *Janelle is covering her face. She doesn't like it when you throw the ball so hard. Let's roll it gently instead.*

Encourage children to problem solve. *You both want the tricycle. What can we do about this?*

Suggest problem-solving strategies. *How about while Marco has a turn on the tricycle, you pretend to be the "traffic light" and say "stop" and "go"? Then you two can switch.*[13]

---

[13] www.zerotothree.org reprinted with permission.

36-Month-Old Milestones

Doctors use certain milestones to tell if a toddler is developing as expected. There's a wide range of what's considered normal, so some children gain skills earlier or later than others. Toddlers who were born prematurely reach milestones later. Always talk with your doctor about your child's progress. Here are some things your toddler might be doing:

Social/Emotional

- ☐ Copies adults and friends
- ☐ Shows affection for friends without prompting
- ☐ Takes turns in games
- ☐ Shows concern for a crying friend
- ☐ Understands the idea of "mine" and "his" or "hers"
- ☐ Shows a wide range of emotions
- ☐ Separates easily from Mom and Dad
- ☐ May get upset with major changes in routine
- ☐ Dresses and undresses self

Language/Communication

- ☐ Follows instructions with 2 or 3 steps
- ☐ Can name most familiar things
- ☐ Understands words like "in," "on," and "under"
- ☐ Says first name, age, and sex
- ☐ Names a friend
- ☐ Says words like "I," "me," "we," and "you" and some plurals (cars, dogs, cats)
- ☐ Talks well enough for strangers to understand most of the time
- ☐ Carries on a conversation using 2 to 3 sentences

Cognitive (learning, thinking, problem-solving)

- ☐ Can work toys with buttons, levers, and moving parts
- ☐ Plays make-believe with dolls, animals, and people
- ☐ Does puzzles with 3 or 4 pieces
- ☐ Understands what "two" means
- ☐ Copies a circle with pencil or crayon
- ☐ Turns book pages one at a time
- ☐ Builds towers of more than 6 blocks
- ☐ Screws and unscrews jar lids or turns door handle

24 TO 36 MONTHS

Movement/Physical Development

☐ Climbs well
☐ Runs easily
☐ Pedals a tricycle (3-wheel bike)
☐ Walks up and down stairs, one foot on each step

You know your child best. Act early if you have concerns about the way your child plays, learns, speaks, acts, or moves, or if your child:

☐ Is missing milestones
☐ Falls down a lot or has trouble with stairs
☐ Drools or has very unclear speech
☐ Can't work simple toys (such as pegboards, simple puzzles, turning handle)
☐ Doesn't speak in sentences
☐ Doesn't understand simple instructions
☐ Doesn't play pretend or make-believe
☐ Doesn't want to play with other children or with toys
☐ Doesn't make eye contact
☐ Loses skills he once had

Tell your child's doctor or nurse if you notice any of these signs of possible developmental delay and ask for a developmental screening.

If you or the doctor is still concerned:

Ask for a referral to a specialist and call any local public elementary school for a free evaluation to find out if your child can get services to help.

For more information, go to **cdc.gov/Concerned**.

*This CDC milestone checklist is not a substitute for a standardized, validated developmental screening tool.

Teaching Your Three-Year-Old

Have a consistent routine for meals, playtime, reading, and bedtime.

Children like to know what to expect. It makes them feel loved and secure, which helps the brain make healthy connections that last a lifetime.

Every day let your child know you love him by a touch, word, or gesture.

Read to your child every day. Ask your child to point to things in the pictures and repeat words after you. **Reading to your child every day is the single most important thing you can do to help them succeed when they start school. Even five minutes a day makes a big difference, but aim for 20 minutes daily.** Try to make it part of your bedtime routine.

Take your child to the library and ask him to help you select the books he wants to read.

During story time, stop in the middle and ask your child what he thinks might happen next. Talk about how the main characters seem to think and feel. Ask him questions: *"What do you see?" "What is happening now?"*

Set rules and limits for your child, and stick to them. If your child breaks a rule, give him a time-out for 30 seconds to one minute in a chair or in his room. Praise your child for following the rules.

Give your child an "activity box" with paper, crayons, and coloring books. Color and draw lines and shapes with your child.

Make a book of words, with pictures, that your child can read. Together, choose ads for familiar stores, restaurants, food, toys, etc. to put in the book.

Play matching games. Ask your child to find objects in books or around the house that are the same.

Teach your child numbers zero through ten. Count steps, toys, and stairs. Count pennies and steps to the door. Count the number of people in the room. When you hand your child crackers, count them out for him. The more you use numbers, the sooner your child will understand that each number corresponds to a certain amount.

24 TO 36 MONTHS

Help your child use counting in daily tasks. "Give everyone three crackers."

Count out loud with your child every time you are walking up steps.

Cut out cardboard feet (by tracing around your child's feet), and number them from one to ten. Arrange them in order and let your child count as he walks on them.

Teach your child how to build a tower using blocks. Playing with blocks helps your child's brain to make important connections necessary for school success. You can use household items like cans, boxes, or books for pretend blocks.

Plan a time every day when you give your child all of your attention. Do whatever he wants to do (even if it is only for ten minutes). This will help him to feel secure and loved.

Tell silly jokes with your child. Laugh with your child. He will have fun when you laugh at his jokes and read books he thinks are funny.

Talk about your child's emotions. For example, say, *"I can tell you feel mad because you threw the puzzle piece."* Encourage your child to identify feelings in books.

Help your child to understand and name his emotions and those of others.

Your child will begin to notice differences between the sexes. Answer your child's questions about differences and similarities between boys and girls in a simple manner.

Play a variety of games with your child. Teach them **"my turn"** and **"your turn"** and **"how to play fair."**

Play catch often with a large lightweight ball. This helps develop many skills necessary for school success.

Play a slow-motion game of *Freeze*. Move slowly, and let your child tell you when to freeze (hold the position), and when to melt (continue moving), stand on one leg while frozen. Take turns.

Give your child the opportunity to climb on equipment both outdoors and indoors. Take your child to a playground. Help him use a variety of equipment: slides, swings, and climbing structures.

To help encourage getting along with others, go to play groups with your child or other places where there are other children,

Work with your child to solve the problem when he is upset.

Let your child help you fold towels and washcloths. Help her feel proud when she gets the edges even.

Make a bird feeder by rolling pine cones in peanut butter and then in bird seed. Hang in your yard and identify the birds that feed there.

Teach your child how to hold a child's pair of safety scissors and how to cut on a line.

Make sure your child knows how to hold a crayon with an adult grip: with thumb on one side, and finger on the other.

Help your child identify colors. Ask your child to group their toys by color. Talk about the colors in your child's clothing as you help him get dressed.

Check out books on colors, numbers, and shapes from the library.

Teach your child basic shapes. Draw a **circle**, a **triangle,** and a **square** and cut them out. Go on a "shape hunt" around the house. Take turns finding circles, triangles, and squares. Let your child make shapes out of Play-Doh.

Make a mask out of a brown grocery bag.

As your child begins to scribble and write, accept all efforts as writing. Encourage them to keep "writing." This is the first step to learning to write letters and words.

Never criticize their efforts at this age.

Let your child watch you write the letters in his name. Ask him if he wants to try.

Praise him no matter what!

Give your child lots of time to use drawing materials on unlined paper.

Encourage your child to draw members of the family, and tell you about the drawings.

Show your child how to fold paper in half to make a simple book. Suggest that she can draw pictures and you will write down the story she tells about them.

Give her containers to play with in the bathtub and the kitchen sink.

Teach your child how to clap to the beat of familiar songs or speech patterns. Show your child how to clap the beat of her name. Compare it to the beat of other family members' names.

24 TO 36 MONTHS

Teach your child nursery rhymes such as *Hickory Dickory Dock, Humpty Dumpty,* or *Jack and Jill*. Experts in literacy and child development have discovered that **if children know eight nursery rhymes by heart by the time they are four years old, they're usually among the best readers by the time they are eight years old.** You can check out a library book that includes all of the popular nursery rhymes or search online.

Play *Simon Says*. Start out with simple directions—"*Simon says, touch your toes*"—then move to silly, more complex routines ("*Simon says, tug on your left ear, then your right ear*"). Variations: You can also encourage your child to jump, skip, catch something, and more.

Take time to observe and describe the weather each day. Introduce words like **rainy, sunny, hot, cold, winter, spring, fall,** and **summer**. Talk to your child each day while you dress him about what kind of clothes are appropriate for the day and why. "*It's very cold out today, so you'll need to wear your hat, scarf, and mittens.*"

Choose a song and have fun repeating it together until she knows it well. This helps her listen to details and remember what she hears.

Give simple three-step instructions to your child and praise them when they succeed. Example: "*Pick up your toys and put them in the bucket and then take the bucket to your room.*"

Every day, have two-way talks about something you saw or did together. Share observations and ideas equally. Ask questions.

Talk to your child about events important to him, such as what happened on his birthday or when he went to visit Grandma.

Ask your child interesting questions that begin with **what**, **how**, and **why**. This gives her practice describing objects, events, and relationships. **Comment on new words when you hear them.** Talk about what they mean. Play a game where you use each new word in a sentence.

Teach them to use these words when asking questions: **is**, **what**, **where**, and **why.**

Use the grocery store as a teaching time. Go to the fresh fruits and vegetables and introduce a new item each visit. Talk about the color, shape, and taste of each fruit or vegetable.

Make a pattern using toothpicks, dry cereal pieces, or coins, and have your child copy it. **Spotting patterns** is another pre-reading skill.

Play outside with your child every week. Go to the park or hiking trail. Allow your child to play freely and without structured activities.

Make a picnic and eat lunch outside. Look at the clouds and ask your child what their shapes remind them of.

Buy sidewalk chalk at the dollar store and play hopscotch on the driveway or sidewalk or draw on black construction paper.

Wash the car and play with the hose and/or sprinkler.

Buy a kiddie pool for fun outdoor play on a hot summer day.

Walk around the block and talk about what you see. Hunt for colors and count how many you can see.

Look at family photos together and name each face and tell a funny story about them.

Build a fort with blankets hung over a table. Get a flashlight and go inside and look at a book together.

Make a cardboard ramp for matchbook cars and trucks to slide down.

Go outside and read a book.

Wash windows with water and vinegar.

Make a game of cleaning up.

Start a collection of coins, stamps, stickers, rocks, or other items found in nature.

Call Grandma or Grandpa or other relatives.

Play hide and seek.

Make a balance beam with tape on the floor and help your child walk it. This will help him learn proper balance.

Paint with watercolors.

Get an large empty box from an appliance or home goods store and turn it into a house for your child.

Work a puzzle with your child.

Avoid digital media.

Digital Media Changes the Brain

In the past 15 years, researchers have been releasing alarming statistics on a sharp and steady increase in children's mental illness, which is now reaching epidemic proportions:

- 1 in 5 children have mental health problems
- 43% increase in ADHD
- 37% increase in teen depression
- 100% increase in suicide rates for children 10 to 14 years old

Excessive use of digital media has severe consequences on developing brains.

Pediatricians are alarmed that children from ages zero to five who spend hours and hours a day on phones, tablets, and around TVs **can develop autistic-like symptoms**. Unfortunately, the average child uses more than seven hours and 38 minutes daily of digital media for entertainment.

Doctors Anne-Lise Ducanda and Isabelle Terrasse contend that **heavy doses of screen time affect what would be, in pre-digital times, the natural wiring of a child's brain**. For example, watching a ball move on a screen does not register in a child's brain the same way it does to manipulate and throw a ball. Says Dr. Ducanda: **"The small child's brain cannot develop without this sense of touch."**

"Screen viewing several hours a day prevents the brain from developing and generates behavior problems and relationship problems," report Dr. Ducanda, and Dr. Terrasse.

Child psychiatrist Dr. Victoria Dunckley says in her book *Reset Your Child's Brain* that increasing numbers of parents are struggling with children who are misbehaving without obvious reasons. Some have stopped responding to their names; they avoid eye contact and have become indifferent to the world around them—characteristics of Autism Spectrum Disorder (ASD). Others were developmentally behind for their age.

Revved up and irritable, many children are diagnosed with ADHD, bipolar illness, autism, or other disorders, but don't respond well to treatment. They are then medicated, often with poor results and unwanted side effects.

It is scientifically proven that the brain has the capacity to rewire itself through the environment. Unfortunately, the environment and parenting styles we are providing for our children are **re-wiring their brains in the wrong direction** and contributing to their challenges in everyday life.

Because of this, today's children are being deprived of the fundamentals of a healthy childhood, such as:

- emotionally available parents
- clearly defined limits and guidance
- responsibilities
- balanced nutrition and adequate sleep
- movement outdoors
- creative play
- social interaction
- opportunities for unstructured times and boredom

Instead, children are being served with:

- digitally distracted parents
- indulgent parents who let kids "rule the world"
- a sense of entitlement rather than responsibility
- inadequate sleep and unbalanced nutrition
- sedentary indoor lifestyles and endless stimulation from technological babysitters
- an absence of dull moments and boredom (which keep children from using their imagination or creativity)

How do we fix it?

If we want our children to grow into happy and healthy individuals, we have to wake up and go back to the basics. Occupational therapist Victoria Prooday says it is still possible to make these changes because hundreds of her clients see a change in their children's emotional state within weeks of implementing these recommendations:

- Set limits and remember that you are your child's PARENT, not their friend.
- Give your children a well-balanced lifestyle filled with what they need, not what they want.
- Don't be afraid to say no to your children.
- Provide nutritious food and limit snacking.
- Spend one hour a day playing outside—biking, hiking, fishing, watching birds or insects.
- Have a daily technology-free family dinner.
- Read and talk to your child every day. Be a word giver.
- Involve your child in one chore a day, folding laundry, cleaning up toys, hanging clothes, unpacking groceries, setting the table.
- Implement consistent sleep routines to ensure your child gets plenty of sleep in a technology-free bedroom.
- Teach responsibility and independence.

24 TO 36 MONTHS

- Wait until a child is at least age six before giving access to a tablet, and only if you've set up time and content limits (which is possible on the Amazon Fire Kids Edition).
- Explain to family members and caregivers why these measures are essential to a child's healthy development, durability and well-being.

Don't overprotect your child from small failures that train them to have the skills needed to overcome life's greater challenges. Don't pack your child's backpack, don't carry her backpack, don't bring to school his forgotten lunch box/homework, and don't peel a banana for a five-year-old child. **Teach them the skills rather than do it for them.**

Teach delayed gratification and provide opportunities for "boredom," because boredom is the time when creativity awakens:

- Do not feel responsible for being your child's entertainment crew.
- Do not use technology as a cure for boredom.
- Avoid using technology during meals, in cars, restaurants, and malls. Use these moments as opportunities to train their brains to function under "boredom."
- Help them create a "boredom first aid kit" with activity ideas for "I am bored" times.

Be emotionally available to connect with kids and teach them self-regulation and social skills:

- Turn off your phones until kids are in bed to avoid digital distraction.
- Become your child's emotional coach. Teach them to recognize and deal with frustration and anger.
- Teach greeting, turn-taking, sharing, empathy, table manners, and conversation skills.
- Connect emotionally—smile, hug, kiss, tickle, read, dance, jump, or crawl with your child.

We must make changes in our children's lives before this entire generation of children is medicated and misdiagnosed.[14]

We're the first generation of parents with 24/7 access to phone calls, email, the Internet, and more, right there in our pockets or purses. It can be hard to navigate the connected world we find ourselves in and remember that the digital universe can wait while we interact with our children in the present moment. We as parents need to put down our cell phones and focus more on our children. They *are* more important than the latest work email or what's trending on Twitter. Let's make sure they know it.

---

14 The Silent Tragedy Affecting Today's Children by Victoria Prooday O.T. 2016 <https://yourot.com/parenting-club/2016/5/16/why-our-children-are-so-bored-at-school-cant-wait-and-get-so-easily-frustrated>. Reprinted with permission.

CHAPTER 4

YOUR FOUR-YEAR-OLD

Your Four-Year-Old

Just as it was when he was three, your four-year-old's fantasy life will remain very active. However, he's now learning the difference between reality and make-believe, and he'll be able to move back and forth between the two without confusing them as much. He's also more friendly and talkative and very curious. At four, your child is likely to be especially sensitive to the feelings of others, and enjoys making people happy.

In what ways does your child enjoy making others happy?

What Your Child Can Do	What You Can Do
I am more creative with make-believe play. * I enjoy doing new things. * I like to play "Mom" and "Dad." * I often can't tell what's real and what's make-believe. * I would rather play with other children than by myself.	**Expose your child to lots of new experiences.** Take your child to the zoo and the park. **Help him with his pretend play** by making suggestions and using props. Stimulate his imagination. **Make sure your child has playmates.** Join a play group or invite neighbors, cousins, or other extended family members to play.
Language and communication are thriving. * I know between 4,000 and 6,000 words. * I can say my first and last name. * I know some basic rules of grammar. * I like to tell stories.	**Read to your child every day.** As you are reading, ask him questions: *What do you think will happen next?* **Talk with your child every day.** Ask questions with *who, what, where,* and *how.* **Teach at least one new word a day.** Draw on your child's interests. **Encourage his storytelling.** Ask your child to retell his favorite story.
I will finish preschool and be ready for kindergarten soon. * I understand counting and numbers. * I am beginning to understand time. * I can copy capital letters. * I can use scissors.	**Give him plenty of opportunities to write, draw, cut, and color.** Help him trace numbers and letters. Buy age-appropriate tracing books from the dollar store. **Help him write his name.** Display his printed name where he can see it every day. Ask him to draw a picture about his favorite storybook.
I am able to hop, skip, jump, and catch a ball.	**Give your child plenty of opportunities for outdoor play.** Teach her how to play hopscotch, ride a tricycle, play catch, and jump rope.

Questions About Sexuality

At about the age of four and five, your preschooler also may begin to show an avid interest in basic sexuality, both his own and that of the opposite sex. He may ask where babies come from and about the organs involved in reproduction and elimination. He may want to know how boys' and girls' bodies are different. When confronted with these kinds of questions, answer in simple but correct terminology. A four-year-old, for example, doesn't need to know the details about intercourse, but he should feel free to ask questions, knowing he'll receive direct and accurate answers.

Along with this increased interest in sexuality, he'll probably also play with his own genitals and may even demonstrate an interest in the genitals of other children. This is normal. These are not adult sexual activities but signs of normal curiosity that don't deserve scolding or punishment.

At what point should parents set limits on such exploration? This really is a family matter. It's probably best not to overreact to it at this age, since it's normal if done in moderation. However, children need to learn what's socially appropriate and what's not.

So, for example, you may decide to tell your child:

- Interest in genital organs is healthy and natural.
- Nudity and sexual play in public are not acceptable.
- No other person, including even close friends and relatives, may touch his "private parts." The exceptions to this rule are doctors and nurses during physical examinations and his own parents when they are trying to find the cause of any pain or discomfort he's feeling in the genital area.

At about this same time, your child also may become fascinated with the parent of the opposite sex. A four-year-old girl can be expected to compete with her mother for her father's attention, just as a boy may be vying for his mother's attention. This so-called oedipal behavior is a normal part of personality development at this age and will disappear in time by itself if the parents take it in stride. There's no need to feel either threatened or jealous because of it.

Behavior

Your child will make a big jump from preschool to kindergarten soon, and with it comes growing pains and sometimes frustration. Your encouragement and support can help him accomplish his goals. **Be patient with him and explain that sometimes it takes lots of tries to reach a goal.** Your child will act out periodically. When he does, handle discipline with the same set of rules:

- **Don't say "no" constantly.** If you do, he will stop listening. Use positive words instead. Say, *"Let's jump off the pillows instead of the bed."* Only say no when necessary. Praise him when he does what you want without being told. Give your child as much freedom to explore as possible.

- **Give choices.** Choices allow your child to feel in control of his world. But make the choices limited so they are not overwhelming. Give him two things to choose between. *"Would you like to do a puzzle or read a book after dinner?"* Or *"It's time to clean up. Would you like to pick up your blocks first or gather the toy trucks?"*

- **Make your expectations clear.** Set up rules that are easy to understand and enforce them the same each time. For example, when dinner starts, tell your child that he can't have dessert unless he eats his vegetables.

Facing Frustrations

Children this age may fall apart when they can't do certain activities on their own, like color in the lines, do a puzzle, or put on their shoes. To help prevent these meltdowns, you should:

- **Understand your child's limits**—be aware of what situations might frustrate your child, and suggest your child take time away from difficult tasks.

- **Offer options that might calm your child.** Make yourself aware of activities or behaviors that help your child relax—like taking a short walk, breathing deep, or checking on his pet—and direct him toward the soothing activity when you see his frustration rising. *Remember not to ever use video games, iPads, or screens as a soothing activity.*

- **Teach your child affirmations and say them together each morning.** You can ask your child to say them while he looks at himself in the mirror, or you can ask him to repeat them after you in the car on the way to school. You can help your child overcome a problem by making specific affirmations that address the issue. For example, if your child gets easily frustrated when trying something new, you can teach him the affirmation *"I can do it if I keep trying my best!"* Below are some other examples:

    - I always do my best.
    - I am strong.
    - I am capable.
    - I am brave.
    - I am kind.
    - I am worthy.
    - I am helpful.

- I am a good friend to others.
- I spread joy.
- I am loved.
- I can become whatever I want to be.
- I am joyful.
- I listen to what others are saying
- Today will be a great day!

Notes:

Four-Year-Old Milestones

Doctors use certain milestones to tell if a child is developing as expected. There's a wide range of what's considered normal, so some children gain skills earlier or later than others. Children who were born prematurely reach milestones later. Check the milestones your child has reached by his or her fourth birthday. Take this list with you and talk with your child's doctor at every visit about the milestones your child has reached and what to expect next.

Here are some things your child might be doing:

Social and Emotional

- ☐ Enjoys doing new things
- ☐ Plays "Mom" and "Dad"
- ☐ Is more and more creative with make-believe play
- ☐ Would rather play with other children than by himself
- ☐ Cooperates with other children
- ☐ Often can't tell what's real and what's make-believe
- ☐ Talks about what she likes and what she is interested in

Language/Communication

- ☐ Knows some basic rules of grammar, such as correctly using "he" and "she"
- ☐ Sings a song or says a poem from memory, such as "The Itsy Bitsy Spider" or "The Wheels on the Bus"
- ☐ Tells stories
- ☐ Can say first and last name

Cognitive (learning, thinking, problem-solving)

- ☐ Names some colors and some numbers
- ☐ Understands the idea of counting
- ☐ Starts to understand time
- ☐ Remembers parts of a story
- ☐ Understands the idea of "same" and "different"
- ☐ Draws a person with 2 to 4 body parts
- ☐ Uses scissors
- ☐ Starts to copy some capital letters
- ☐ Plays board or card games
- ☐ Tells you what he thinks is going to happen next in a book

YOUR FOUR-YEAR-OLD

Movement/Physical Development

☐ Hops and stands on one foot up to 2 seconds
☐ Catches a bounced ball most of the time
☐ Pours and cuts with supervision, and mashes own food

Act early and tell your doctor if your child:

☐ Can't jump in place
☐ Has trouble scribbling
☐ Shows no interest in interactive games or make-believe
☐ Ignores other children or doesn't respond to people outside the family
☐ Resists dressing, sleeping, and using the toilet
☐ Can't retell a favorite story
☐ Doesn't follow 3-part commands
☐ Doesn't understand "same" and "different"
☐ Doesn't use "me" and "you" correctly
☐ Speaks unclearly
☐ Loses skills he once had

Tell your child's doctor or nurse if you notice any of these signs of possible developmental delay and ask for a developmental screening.

If you or the doctor is still concerned:

Ask for a referral to a specialist and call any local public elementary school for a free evaluation to find out if your child can get services to help.

For more information, go to **cdc.gov/Concerned**.

* This CDC milestone checklist is not a substitute for a standard, validated developmental screening tool.

Teaching Your Four-Year-Old

A four-year-old has a vocabulary of 4,000 to 6,000 words and is learning an average of five new words a day! **Help your child develop language skills by talking to him every day about a new word.** Play a game where you each use the new word in a sentence.

Ask your child interesting questions that start with **what**, **how,** and **why**. This gives him practice describing things.

Talk to your child about events important to him, such as what happened on his birthday or when he went to Grandma's house.

Every day have two-way talks about what you saw or did together. Share observations and ideas equally.

Spend some time each night talking with your child about things that happened **yesterday**, **today,** and what might happen **tomorrow**.

Read a story to your child every day. Aim for 20 minutes daily. Stop in the middle of the story and ask what your child thinks will happen next. Talk about the facial expressions and emotions of the characters. Teach your child to handle emotions and discuss how everyone has times when they feel **happy**, **sad**, **tired**, **bored**, **excited**, or **frustrated**.

Put your child's name on many things: her books, the door to her room, her bag.

Ask your child to tell a story about a picture. Write what he says below the picture. Read it back to him. Let him "read" it. Put the picture on the wall in his room.

Help your child learn to write his name. Praise his efforts no matter what.

Teach grouping. Help your child understand that some things go together because they look, feel, sound, or taste the same. For instance, a fork, knife, and spoon all go together because they are used together. And an apple, firetruck, and valentine could be grouped together because they are all the same color. Play a game by asking, ***"Which of these is not like the others?"***
Examples:
An apple, banana, orange, and egg.
A shirt, pants, socks, and pencil.
A crayon, marker, pencil, and flashlight.

At the grocery store, point out how things are organized: *fresh fruit and vegetables here, books and magazines there, and frozen foods over there.* Continue teaching him about new fruits and vegetables from the produce section when shopping.

When you get home from the store, let your child help you figure out where to put the things you bought. Talk about why they belong where you put them.

Collect a set of five buttons, coins, or circles of paper of varying sizes. Ask your child to find the smallest one. Then arrange the rest in order from smallest to largest, left to right. Discuss what you have done. Now mix the objects up and ask your child to find the largest and arrange the rest from largest to smallest.

Help your child make a book of colors. Pick a color each week and ask your child to notice all of the things he sees that are that color. Let him wear clothes of that color for the week.

Use coins to make patterns. Name the coins as you or your child set up a pattern: *penny, penny, nickel, penny, penny, nickel...*

Play board games in which you have to count the squares to move ahead. Borrow counting books from the library. Help your child make his own counting book.

Help your child understand time by using these words often: **first, next, last, after, before, tomorrow,** and **yesterday**. Help your child think about each step in an activity, and how they go in a certain order. For example, when we wash our hair: **First** we wet our hair. **Then** we put some shampoo in our hand. **Next** we soap and scrub our head and hair, and **lastly** we rinse away the shampoo.
What do we take off first, our socks or our shoes?
I put on my coat. What do you think I'll do next?
When you get dressed in the morning, what do you put on last?
Talk about what you did *yesterday* and what you will do *tomorrow*.

Help your child behave better by preparing her when it's time to change an activity: *"In a few minutes I'm going to call you to pick up your toys so we can go to the store, so finish your game."*

Let your child decide what to wear, when possible.

Ask your child what their favorites are: food, color, animal, toy, place, game.

Say "**please**" and "**thank you**" to your child. Modeling polite manners will teach him. Give him gentle reminders without embarrassing him in front of others.

Offer to count how many times your child can bounce and catch a ball before he misses. Write the number and post it on the refrigerator. Can he beat his score?

Your Child's First Teacher *Is You*

Help your child set up "targets" such as a laundry basket or trash can turned on its side to kick a ball into. Stand near the target so you can return the ball after he tries to "score." Count up his "points."

Be sure to take your child to a playground several times every week. At this age, he needs lots of exercise and plenty of chances to run, jump, climb, and swing.

Use a calendar to help your child count off how many days in a month until his birthday or other special event.

Cook with your child. Ask her to help you measure the ingredients to your favorite cookie or dessert recipe. Teach her measurement words such as **cup**, **teaspoon,** and **tablespoon**.

Let your child pour his drink from a light pitcher that doesn't have very much in it.

Stargaze at the night sky.

Paint a flower pot and plant some seeds. Your child will love watching them grow. You can buy inexpensive, simple herb-growing kits at the drug store.

Notes:

_____
_____
_____
_____
_____
_____
_____
_____
_____
_____
_____
_____
_____
_____
_____
_____
_____

Notes:

CHAPTER 5

YOUR FIVE-YEAR-OLD

Your Five-Year-Old

The world gets larger for a five-year-old when they enter kindergarten. For some children school is exciting, and for others it is overwhelming. It's important to make sure that your child is happy and secure in their new world. Allow them to be independent when they want to be, but be sure to give them plenty of hugs and encouragement too. They are entering the "big kid" world of better emotional control, and many of them are "people pleasers" who want to make new friends and receive plenty of praise from the adults in their life.

What does your child like and dislike about school?

What Your Child Can Do	What You Can Do
In school I am learning to recognize numbers and letters, learning to write, read, and do simple math. * This is an exciting time, but also overwhelming. * I may need extra reassurance from you as I adjust to the challenges of school.	**Begin introducing numbers, letters, and writing at home.** Provide plenty of books and writing materials. Visit the library weekly to check out new books and read to your child daily. Play simple math games with your child. Count, sort, and group objects such as blocks or toys.
I am becoming more social and high energy and enjoy play dates with friends as well as team sports. * I enjoy spending time with other children and like to play outdoors more. * I prefer activities that involve other children. * My increased ability to balance and coordinate movements allows me to ride a bike, swim, jump rope, and perform most ball-related skills.	**Enroll your child in team sports** through the Troup County Parks and Recreation Department. **Plan play dates with your child's friends** at church or school. **Visit the playground weekly.**
I like new experiences, enjoy the challenges of problem-solving, and ask more questions. * I like to think of imaginative ways to do a task, make something, or solve a problem. * I ask more questions about how and why things work because I want to understand more. * I love to "investigate." * I weigh my choices more carefully now.	**Follow your child's interest and take them to museums, exhibits, and on nature treks often.** Check out books from the library on subjects your child is interested in. **Give your child plenty of exposure to a variety of topics such as science, nature, art, crafts, and sports activities.** Hands-on experiences help to form theories to explain "how" and "why" things happen. Help your child carry out simple investigations such as science experiments.

YOUR FIVE-YEAR-OLD

What Your Child Can Do	What You Can Do
My language skills are well developed now. * I can pronounce words clearly, speak in complex sentences, and use correct grammar. * I have a good-size vocabulary that continues to grow rapidly. * In conversation, I can wait my turn to speak. * I can include appropriate details when sharing a personal experience.	**Have a conversation with your child every day.** Ask your child questions about his day, comment on what is happening, discuss the weather and your child's particular interests. As you read together, discuss as you go. Ask lots of questions. *What do you think will happen next? Who is your favorite character? Why do you think he did that?*

Five-year-olds begin to extend their language skills from talking to reading and writing. They know their uppercase and most lowercase letters and understand that letters represent specific sounds in spoken words. This knowledge helps them to sound out words in print and write out words based on their sounds. They also can discuss stories and are able to tell their own tales.

They can count out a collection of up to 20 items, do simple addition and subtraction, and identify which number in a set is larger. Five-year-olds understand and use words related to position, such as "under" or "behind." They sequence events in their correct order and are learning to tell time. They can also sort objects based on more than one characteristic.

Children this age can manage feelings and social situations with greater independence. They might decide on their own to go to another room to calm down, or try strategies like negotiation and compromise to resolve a conflict before seeking adult help. They also have improved skills for forming and maintaining friendships with adults and other children. Being accepted by "the group" is becoming more and more important.

In the creative arts, five-year-olds love music and enjoy trying to make their own music. They create realistic art with recognizable subjects and more details. They also recognize that art can tell a story. The dramatic play of five-year-olds is pre-planned and elaborate. They are able to perform simple plays, do pantomime, and perform puppet shows.

Five-year-olds should be doing chores around the house. Studies show that children who do weekly chores are better adjusted, more confident, and do better in school. Ask your child to help put away the groceries, make their bed, fold laundry, put their toys and shoes away, or help take care of pets.

Five-Year-Old Milestones

Doctors use certain milestones to tell if a child is developing as expected. There's a wide range of what's considered normal, so some children gain skills earlier or later than others. Children who were born prematurely reach milestones later. Check the milestones your child has reached by his or her fifth birthday. Take this list with you and talk with your child's doctor at every visit about the milestones your child has reached and what to expect next.

Here are some things your five-year-old might be doing:

Social and Emotional

- ☐ Wants to please friends
- ☐ Wants to be like friends
- ☐ More likely to agree with rules
- ☐ Likes to sing, dance, and act
- ☐ Is aware of gender
- ☐ Can tell what's real and what's make-believe
- ☐ Shows more independence (for example, may visit a next-door neighbor by himself [adult supervision is still needed])
- ☐ Is sometimes demanding and sometimes very cooperative

Language/Communication

- ☐ Speaks very clearly
- ☐ Tells a simple story using full sentences
- ☐ Uses future tense; for example, "Grandma will be here."
- ☐ Says name and address

Cognitive (learning, thinking, problem-solving)

- ☐ Counts 10 or more things
- ☐ Can draw a person with at least 6 body parts
- ☐ Can print some letters or numbers
- ☐ Copies a triangle and other geometric shapes
- ☐ Knows about things used every day, like money and food

YOUR FIVE-YEAR-OLD

Movement/Physical Development

☐ Stands on one foot for 10 seconds or longer
☐ Hops; may be able to skip
☐ Can do a somersault
☐ Uses a fork and spoon and sometimes a table knife
☐ Can use the toilet on her own
☐ Swings and climbs

Act early by talking to your child's doctor if your child:

☐ Doesn't show a wide range of emotions
☐ Shows extreme behavior (unusually fearful, aggressive, shy, or sad)
☐ Unusually withdrawn and not active
☐ Is easily distracted, has trouble focusing on one activity for more than 5 minutes
☐ Doesn't respond to people, or responds only superficially
☐ Can't tell what's real and what's make-believe
☐ Doesn't play a variety of games and activities
☐ Can't give first and last name
☐ Doesn't use plurals or past tense properly
☐ Doesn't talk about daily activities or experiences
☐ Doesn't draw pictures
☐ Can't brush teeth, wash and dry hands, or get undressed without help
☐ Loses skills he once had

Tell your child's doctor or nurse if you notice any of these signs of possible developmental delay and ask for a developmental screening.

If you or the doctor is still concerned:

Ask for a referral to a specialist and call any local public elementary school for a free evaluation to find out if your child can get services to help.

For more information, go to **cdc.gov/Concerned**.

*This CDC milestone checklist is not a substitute for a standardized, validated developmental screening tool.

Teaching Your Five-Year-Old

At age five, your child should have a vocabulary of 5,000 to 8,000 words and be learning an average of five new words a day. **Have conversations with your child more often than you give him directions.** Have conversations with your child during meals, in the car, waiting in line. He will learn words and grammar from daily interaction with family.

Read with your child every day for at least 20 minutes. Choose books that contain some words your child may know, and talk about what the words mean.

Tell a true story together. Ask your child to help you tell someone else about something you saw or something funny that happened.

Take your child to the library and let him select books he likes. Borrow or buy a book at least as often as you borrow or buy a video. Books introduce vocabulary that often isn't used in daily life.

Occasionally read out letters as you read aloud to your child.

Label some things in your house with big, clear words.

Make an alphabet book or letter scrapbook.

Give your child four simple, related directions in order. Example: *"Put your shoes on, grab your coat, zip it up, and get your ball so we can go play."* This is an important skill he will need for school.

Give your child a weekly job: feed the dog, make his bed, clear the table. **Studies show children who have chores do better in school, are better adjusted, and get along well with others.**

Help your child feel confident enough to try again when he makes a mistake. **Teach him that mistakes are an opportunity for learning.** Praise him when he tries again.

Enjoy simple games together: card games, board games, ball games. This is great practice for helping him understand rules, how to play fair, and winning and losing.

Have a conversation with your child about something that interests him. He should be able to respond to your conversation for seven turns on the same topic. This helps his attention span.

After you read a story together, ask your child to tell you the story he just heard. Let him hold the book and look at the pictures to help prompt him. If he gets stuck, ask him, *"What is happening in this picture?"*

Put on music and see if your child can find and clap to the beat of the music by himself.

Read a book together on colors. Can your child name the eight basic colors? **Red, orange, yellow, green, blue, purple, brown,** and **black.**

Use a few leftover cooked spaghetti noodles, dip them in paint, and move the noodles around on paper to paint an abstract painting.

Dip the wheels of a few small cars or trucks in different colors of paint and roll them on paper to make a creative art piece.

Put a piece of paper in a box or a box top. Drip two or three different colors of paint on the paper, add four or five marbles, and roll them around for more creative artwork.

Teach your child his left and right hands and feet. Talk about being right handed and left handed.

Play games with your child such as *Simon Says* and *Follow the Leader*. Take turns being the leader and tell your child to balance on one foot. At this age he should be able to hold it for ten seconds. Next, ask him to hop on one foot. Also try jumping, skipping, and somersaults.

Use your child's toys to play number and sorting games. Ask him to count out ten toys. Then ask him to sort his toys by size, shape, length, category, and color (grouping by only one of these at a time).

Sculpt the alphabet with Play-Doh.

Explore how water travels through leaves by adding some red food coloring to water and snipping the end of the leaf and placing it in the water. Watch it over the next few days to see how the leaf absorbs water.

Use toothpicks and marshmallows to create unique structures for play.

Make sure your child knows his full name and address. He should also memorize your cell phone number. Write his name on many things at home and be sure he can recognize it before he begins school. Teach him how to write his first name.

Play the "I Spy ABC's" game. Look for letters when you are outside, riding in the car, at the store, or around your neighborhood.

Fill the bottom of two-liter plastic soda bottles with water and use as bowling pins.

Go on a treasure hunt outside. Take a small bag and have your child collect things in nature that he finds interesting, such as beautiful leaves, rocks, or pine cones. Make a display of them in his room. Follow his interests.

Draw your favorite songs. As you sing one of your child's favorite songs, draw a simple picture of what is happening in the lyrics, then hand your child the paper to draw something else mentioned in the song. For example, if you are singing "The Wheels on the Bus," draw the bus, and then let your child draw the wheels. Go back and forth drawing until the song ends.

Melt ice using salt. Freeze water overnight in plastic bowls. Have your child pour a small amount of salt over the ice. Use eyedroppers to add the watercolor so they can see the ravines that the salt has made in the ice.

For additional activities, read over the **Kindergarten Readiness Checklist** in the following section to determine which skills your child may need help mastering.

Behavior

Teach your child ways to control his temper. He can use words to express his feelings, go into another room, or start a new activity. Model these actions to control your own temper.

Help your child behave well in public. For example, prepare him before going into a movie: remind him of the need to listen quietly. Explain to him why: he will be able to listen better, and so will others.

Make sure your child has plenty of experience using manners too. Teach him how to share, take turns, how to be a good winner and loser, how to compromise and to always say "please" and "thank you." These are very important social skills to master before entering kindergarten.

Children learn their social skills from their parents. Their attitudes toward life and school come from what you do and say. Be mindful of your attitudes toward these things.

For more tips on controlling behavior, read Chapter Six.

A Kindergarten Readiness Checklist

Did you know that six out of ten children are unprepared for kindergarten? In a survey conducted by D. Keith Osborn, a professor of child development and education at the University of Georgia, more than 3,000 kindergarten teachers in the United States and Canada were asked to list what skills children need in order to be ready for entering kindergarten. While Osborn stresses that your child does not need to master every one of these skills, the following is a sampling of what teachers think a beginning kindergartner should be able to do:

Verbal Skills:

- ☐ Speaks clearly; can be easily understood by others
- ☐ Speaks in sentences
- ☐ Uses appropriate volume when speaking
- ☐ Can express and describe feelings

Listening Skills:

- ☐ Listens with understanding of directions
- ☐ Can follow one- and two-step directions

Reading Readiness:

- ☐ Listens well when read to
- ☐ Shows interest in reading related activities
- ☐ Understands left to right movement of reading
- ☐ Retells information from a story
- ☐ Can put 3 pictures from a story in the correct order
- ☐ Uses imagination

Alphabet:

- ☐ Recites the alphabet
- ☐ Recognizes capital and lowercase letters
- ☐ Matches capital letters with lowercase letters
- ☐ Identifies the sound each letter makes

Writing:

- ☐ Likes to scribble or draw
- ☐ Traces letters and numbers
- ☐ Writes a few letters or numbers without tracing

Gross Motor Skills:

- ☐ Runs
- ☐ Skips
- ☐ Hops on both feet and on one foot
- ☐ Gallops
- ☐ Leaps
- ☐ Jumps
- ☐ Climbs a playground ladder
- ☐ Throws a ball with direction
- ☐ Catches a thrown ball with arms and body
- ☐ Bounces a ball
- ☐ Pedals and steers a tricycle
- ☐ Can turn a somersault

Fine Motor Skills:

- ☐ Grasps a crayon or pencil correctly
- ☐ Can copy lines, circles, squares, and triangles
- ☐ Can stack 10 one-inch blocks
- ☐ Can zip pants
- ☐ Can button shirt
- ☐ Can lace string
- ☐ Can string beads
- ☐ Can snap fingers
- ☐ Can complete a puzzle with 7 or more pieces
- ☐ Can use child scissors
- ☐ Completes a simple pattern
- ☐ Uses glue neatly
- ☐ Can make a ball, snake, or pancake using Play-Doh

Math:

- ☐ Counts objects to 10
- ☐ Counts to 20
- ☐ Can match numbers (5 apples to the numeral 5)

- ☐ Can sort items by color, shape, and size
- ☐ Can recognize a simple pattern and duplicate it (such as black, white, black, white, or large, small, large, small)
- ☐ Can identify a circle, square, triangle, and rectangle
- ☐ Can put in order several objects based on one attribute (such as, which of these is red? Or which of these do we use in the kitchen?)
- ☐ Understands directions such as up/down, left/right, fast/slow, long/short
- ☐ Understands comparative words such as big/little, noisy/quiet, easy/hard

Creative Arts:

- ☐ Identifies these colors: red, yellow, blue, green, orange, purple, black, white, brown, and pink
- ☐ Explores different art materials
- ☐ Draws lines and shapes
- ☐ Interprets pictures

Music and Movement:

- ☐ Participates in group music experiences
- ☐ Dances to music
- ☐ Sings
- ☐ Plays simple instruments

Creative Drama:

- ☐ Make-believes with objects
- ☐ Takes on pretend roles or situations

Self-knowledge:

- ☐ Knows first and last name
- ☐ Correctly states his/her gender and age
- ☐ Knows address and phone number
- ☐ Knows names of parents
- ☐ Knows birthday

Interaction with Others:

- ☐ Plays well with others
- ☐ Takes turns and shares
- ☐ Cleans up after playing
- ☐ Participates in group activities

- ☐ Interacts easily with familiar adults
- ☐ Listens when others speak
- ☐ Uses manners
- ☐ Considerate of other people's feelings
- ☐ Seeks adult help during conflicts

Approach to Learning:

- ☐ Is pleasant and cooperative
- ☐ Shows eagerness and curiosity
- ☐ Is persistent in tasks
- ☐ Seeks help with problems

Health and Wellness:

- ☐ Knows how to wash hands
- ☐ Follows proper bathroom procedures
- ☐ Can put shoes and coat on independently
- ☐ Brushes teeth independently
- ☐ Can dress appropriately for the weather
- ☐ Distinguishes between healthy and non-healthy foods

Self-Control:

- ☐ Follows rules and procedures
- ☐ Able to move from one activity to the next without problems
- ☐ Expresses self with words, rather than acting out physically
- ☐ Demonstrates normal activity level

Notes:

CHAPTER 6
COMMON PARENTING MISTAKES

Common Parenting Mistakes and How to Fix Them

Victoria Prooday, an occupational therapist based in Canada, says she hears the same consistent message from every teacher she meets. "Kids today are impatient, bored, friendless, and entitled. Most come to school emotionally unavailable for learning. I have seen and continue to see a decline in children's social, emotional, and academic functioning, as well as a sharp increase in learning disabilities and other diagnoses."

There are many factors in our modern lifestyle that contribute to this. "As we know," says Prooday, "the brain is malleable. Through environment, we can make the brain 'stronger' or make it 'weaker.' I truly believe that, despite all our greatest intentions, we unfortunately remold our children's brains in the wrong direction."

Here is why:

1. KIDS GET EVERYTHING THEY WANT WHEN THEY WANT IT

"I'm hungry!"—*"In a sec I will stop at the drive-thru."*
"I'm thirsty!"—*"Here is a vending machine."*
"I'm bored!"—*"Use my phone!"*

The ability to **delay gratification** is one of the key factors for future success. We have the best intentions—to make our child happy—but unfortunately, **we make them happy at the moment but miserable in the long term.** To be able to delay gratification means to be able to function under stress. Our children are gradually becoming less equipped to deal with even minor stressors, which eventually become huge obstacles to their success in life.

The inability to delay gratification is often seen in classrooms, malls, restaurants, and toy stores the moment the child hears "No," because parents have taught their child's brain to get what it wants right away.

2. LIMITED SOCIAL INTERACTION

We are all busy, so we give our children digital gadgets and make them "busy" too. Kids <u>used to play outside, where, in unstructured natural environments, they learned and practiced their social skills.</u> Unfortunately, technology replaced the outdoor time. Also, technology made the parents less available to socially interact with their child. Obviously, our kids fall behind. The babysitting gadget is not equipped to help kids develop social skills. Most successful people have great social skills. This is the priority.

The brain is just like a muscle that is trainable and re-trainable. If you want your child to be able to bike, you teach him biking skills. If you want your child to be able to wait, you need to teach that child patience. If you want your child to be able to socialize, you need to teach him social skills. The same applies to all the other skills. There is no difference.

3. ENDLESS FUN

We have created an artificial fun world for our children. There are no dull moments. The moment it becomes quiet, we run to entertain them again, because otherwise, we feel that we are not doing our parenting duty. We live in two separate worlds. They have their "fun" world, and we have our "work" world. Why aren't children helping us in the kitchen or with laundry? Why don't they tidy up their toys? This is basic monotonous work that trains the brain to be workable and function under "boredom," which is the same "muscle" that is required to be eventually teachable at school. When they come to school and it is time for handwriting, their answer is "I can't. It is too hard. Too boring." Why? Because the workable "muscle" is not getting trained through endless fun. It gets trained through work.

4. TECHNOLOGY

Using technology as a free babysitting service is, in fact, not free at all. The payment is waiting for you just around the corner. We pay with our kids' nervous systems, with their attention, and with their ability for delayed gratification. Compared to virtual reality, everyday life is boring. When kids come to the classroom, they are exposed to human voices and adequate visual stimulation as opposed to being bombarded with the graphic explosions and special effects that they are used to seeing on the screens. **After hours of virtual reality, processing information in a classroom becomes increasingly challenging for our kids because their brains are getting used to the high levels of stimulation that video games provide.** The inability to process lower levels of stimulation leaves kids vulnerable to academic challenges. Technology also disconnects us emotionally from our children and our families. **Parental emotional availability is the main nutrient for a child's brain.** Unfortunately, we are gradually depriving our children of that nutrient.

5. KIDS RULE THE WORLD

"My son doesn't like vegetables." "She doesn't like going to bed early." "He doesn't like to eat breakfast." "She doesn't like toys, but she is very good at her iPad." "He doesn't want to get dressed on his own." "She is too lazy to eat on her own." This is what we hear from parents all the time. Since when do children dictate to us how to parent them? If we leave it all up to them, all they are going to do is eat junk food, watch TV, play on their tablets, and never go to bed. What good are we doing them by giving them what they WANT when we know that it is not GOOD for them?

Without proper nutrition and a good night's sleep, our kids come to school irritable, anxious, and inattentive. In addition, we send them the wrong message. They learn they can do what they want and not do what they don't want. The concept of "need to do" is absent. Unfortunately, in order to achieve our goals in life, we have to do what's necessary, which may not always be what we want to do. For example, if a child wants to be an "A" student, he needs to study hard. If he wants to be a successful soccer player, he needs to practice every day. Our children know very well what they want, but have a very hard time doing what is necessary to achieve that goal. This results in unattainable goals and leaves the child disappointed.

Train Their Brain for Success

You can make such a difference in your child's life by training your child's brain so that he will successfully function on social, emotional, and academic levels. Here is how:

1. Don't be afraid to set limits. Kids need limits to grow happy and healthy.

- Make a schedule for mealtime, sleep time, technology time—and stick to it.
- Think of what is GOOD for them—not what they WANT/DON'T WANT. Parenting is a hard job. You need to be creative to make them do what is good for them, because, most of the time, that is the exact opposite of what they want.
- Kids need breakfast and nutritious food. They need to spend time outdoors and go to bed at a consistent time in order to come to school available for learning the next day. Convert things that they don't like doing/trying into fun, emotionally stimulating games.
- Discipline your children. Have rules and stick to them. **Most parents don't realize that there is an important period during the first four or five years of a child's life when he can be taught proper attitudes and discipline. These early ideas become rather permanent. When those years have passed, it is more difficult to discipline or control a child's behavior.**

2. Limit technology, and reconnect with your kids emotionally

- Surprise them with flowers, share a smile, tickle them, put a love note in their backpack or under their pillow.
- Give your child plenty of praise and encouragement. ***Find at least one thing to praise your child for every day.*** Example: *I like the way you put things away without being asked.* Or *I like the way you always help me with chores.* Give him a word of praise every time he behaves the way you would like him to. Teachers know the trick of praising good behavior and ignoring bad behavior. Eventually the child realizes that they get more attention when they are behaving the way you would like them to.
- Surprise them by taking them out for lunch on a school day.
- Dance together, crawl together, have pillow fights.
- Have family dinners, and regular board or card game nights.
- Go biking, go on outdoor walks with a flashlight in the evening.
- **Be emotionally available for your children: it is the main nutrient for a child's brain.**

3. Train delayed gratification

- Make them wait! It is okay to have *"I am bored"* time. This is where creativity and imagination come into play.

- Gradually increase the waiting time between "I want" and "I get."
- Avoid technology use in cars and restaurants, and instead teach them waiting while talking and playing games.
- Limit constant snacking.

4. Teach your child to do monotonous work from their early years as it is the foundation for future "workability."

- Chores such as folding laundry, tidying up toys, hanging clothes, unpacking groceries, setting the table, making lunch, unpacking their lunch box, and making their bed give children more self-worth, independence, and make them feel "grown up."
- Be creative. Initially, make it stimulating and fun so that their brain associates it with something positive.
- Studies show that children who have chores have more self-confidence, are better adjusted, and do better in school than children who don't.

5. Teach social skills. Be sure to teach your children:

- How to take turns
- How to share
- How to be a good winner and a good loser
- How to compromise
- How to compliment others
- How to use **please** and **thank you**

Talk to your children every day, not just AT them. Try to answer your child's questions in a way that will be meaningful. If you dodge a question or give a vague, uninterested answer, he will pick up on this, and soon his natural curiosity will be gone, sometimes forever. During conversations with your child, ask him questions such as:

Why do you think that happened?
How did you do that?
What do you think about this?
What are you doing now?
How does that make you feel?

Provide a sense of family history for your child by telling positive stories and passing on family history. Talk to your child about values such as:

Honesty—when we break something, we admit our mistake and apologize
Kindness—we take turns, help others, and say "please" and "thank you"
Hard work—it is the secret to success and happiness

A sense of humor—we find something to laugh at every day
Giving to others—every day we try to give a smile, a helping hand, and a kind word

Children learn their social skills from their parents. Their attitudes toward life and school come from what you do and say. Be mindful of your attitudes toward these things.[15]

6. Build on your child's interests. With a little encouragement on your part, one simple interest of your child's can blossom into a source of knowledge and responsibility in which your child can shine. For example: if your child enjoys playing outside, help him notice interesting sights and sounds in nature.

Go to the library and find children's books on topics that interest him. Regular trips to the library are the best way to ensure your child will learn to read. The librarian can help you select age-appropriate books for your child. You can check out as many as 50 books at a time and keep them for two weeks before they are due. Just two trips to the library a month will give your child plenty of free books to look at every day!

LaGrange Memorial Library
115 Alford Street
LaGrange, Georgia
706 882-7784
Hours: Monday—Tuesday 9:00 am to 8:00 pm
Wednesday—Thursday 9:00 am to 7:00 pm
Friday—9:00 am to 5:00 pm
Saturday—10:00 am to 5:00 pm
Closed Sundays. Children's story time is on Wednesday at 10:30 followed by craft time.

In addition to the library, take your child to the museum or historical areas near your home. This makes learning fun and awakens your child's natural curiosity. It will instill a love of learning for its own sake. Here are some local attractions:

LaGrange Art Museum
112 LaFayette Parkway
LaGrange, Georgia
706 882-3267
The museum offers many programs for children on Saturdays and throughout the summer months and has a monthly art exhibit. For more information visit: lagrangeartmuseum.org.

---

15   Why Kids are Impatient, Bored, Friendless and Entitled by Victoria Prooday. 2016 < https://yourot.com/parenting-club/2016/5/16/why-our-children-are-so-bored-at-school-cant-wait-and-get-so-easily-frustrated>.   Reprinted   with permission.

Explorations in Antiquity Center
130 Gordon Commercial Drive
LaGrange, Georgia
706 885-0363
Hours: Tuesday—Saturday 10:00 to 6:00
The Antiquity Center takes you back to biblical times. Here you can explore replicas of tombs which carry the burial remains of Jesus and Abraham. The museum also displays a city wall and a village dating back nearly 2,000 years.

Troup County Archives and Legacy Museum
136 Main Street
LaGrange, Georgia
706 884-1828
In less than an hour you can learn all about the history and making of LaGrange. Some exhibits and hands-on items are for children. For more information visit trouparchives.org.

Implementing these ideas can help your child's behavior sooner than you might think. Children will change the moment parents change their perspective on parenting. Remember that **early habits last a lifetime.** Help your children succeed in life by training and strengthening their brain now. After all, **you are your child's first and best teacher.**

Bibliography

Ames, Louise Bates. *Your Four-Year-Old: Wild and Wonderful.* Dell Books, November 1, 1989.

Ames, Louise Bates. *Your Five-Year-Old: Sunny and Serene.* Dell Books, February 15, 1989.

ChuChu TV Studios. "Is Using Phone While Breastfeeding Dangerous for the Baby?" February 14, 2018. http://chuchutv.com/blog/is-using-phone-while-breastfeeding-dangerous-for-the-baby/

Gritt, Emma. "Checking Your Phone While Breastfeeding Is Harmful To Your Baby." September 29, 2015. https://www.thesun.co.uk/archives/news/182539/checking-your-phone-while-breastfeeding-is-harmful-to-your-baby/

Hagan, Joseph Jr., Shaw, Judith S, Duncan, Paula M. *Bright Futures: Guidelines for Health Supervision of Infants, Children and Adolescents.* Third Edition. 2008, Elk Grove Village, IL: American Academy of Pediatrics.

Kelly, Marguerite, Parsons, Elia. *The Mother's Almanac Revised.* Broadway Books, 1992.

Lukken, Miriam. *Read This Book Before Your Child Starts School.* Charles C. Thomas, 1994.

Park, Alice. "Cell Phone Distracted Parenting Can Have Long-Term Consequences." *Time Magazine.* 6 January 2016.

Pediatrics & Child Health, Community Pediatrics Committee, Canadian Pediatric Society, (2000) "Toilet Learning: Anticipatory Guidance With a Child-Oriented Approach." 5(6), 333-335.

Parlakian, Rebecca, Lerner, Claire. Zero to Three: National Center for Infants, Toddlers, and Families; copyright 2013 video: Brain Development from Birth-Magic of Everyday Moments.

Prooday, Victoria. "The Silent Tragedy Affecting Today's Children." 2016 https://yourot.com/parenting-club/2016/5/16/why-our-children-are-so-bored-at-school-cant-wait-and-get-so-easily-frustrated

Prooday, Victoria. "Why Kids Are Impatient, Bored, Friendless and Entitled." 2016 https://yourot.com/parenting-club/2016/5/16/why-our-children-are-so-bored-at-school-cant-wait-and-get-so-easily-frustrated

Shelov, Steven, Remer Altmann, Tanya. *Your Baby's First Year* and *Caring for Your Baby and Young Child: Birth to Age 5.* Fifth Edition © 1991, 1993, 1998, 2004, 2009 by the American Academy of Pediatrics.

Woolf, A., Kenna, M., and Shane, H., Eds. *Children's Hospital Guide to Your Child's Health and Development.* Children's Hospital Boston, Cambridge, MA: Perseus Books, 2001.

Appendix

BABIES LEARNING ON COURSE FOR KINDERGARTEN SUCCESS

An early childhood education initiative in West Georgia

We are working hard to ensure every child is fully prepared for kindergarten.

Our four-prong strategy to achieve our vision:

Awareness — Spreading awareness to all families of the importance of early learning.

Connection — Connecting families with early learning opportunities in our community.

Collaboration — Supporting quality improvement among community organizations, government, and childcare providers.

Expansion — Promoting the increase in quantity and quality of early learning opportunities in West Georgia.

For more information visit us at:

blockswga.org

GEORGIA'S BABIES CAN'T WAIT PROGRAM
Purpose of the Program

1. Provide a coordinated, comprehensive, and integrated system of services for infants and toddlers with special needs, birth to 3, and their families.
2. Provide early identification and screening of children with developmental delays and chronic health conditions.
3. Improve the developmental potential of infants and toddlers, birth to age 3, with developmental or chronic health conditions.

What does the program do?

Babies Can't Wait: Part C early intervention builds upon and provides support and resources to assist family members and caregivers to enhance children's learning and development through everyday learning opportunities.

Why is the program important?

This program enhances the capacity of families to meet the special needs of their child in order to ensure that each young child with significant developmental delays achieves his or her maximum developmental potential.

What services does BCW provide?

- Multidisciplinary evaluation to determine eligibility and multidisciplinary assessments to determine the scope of services needed.
- Service coordination that assists the family and other professionals in developing a plan to enhance the child's development.

Note: The above two services are offered to families at NO cost.

- Access to early intervention services identified in the child's Individualized Family Service Plan (IFSP). State funds are available, based on a sliding fee scale, to assist families who are determined by the local BCW program to be unable to pay.

What are early intervention services?

Services may include assistive technology devices and services, audiology services, family training, counseling, and home visits, health services, medical diagnostic services, certain nursing services, nutrition services, occupational therapy, physical therapy, psychological services, social work services, special instruction, speech-language pathology, vision services, and transportation and related costs.

Where are early intervention services provided?

Services are provided in natural environments, including home and community settings in which children without disabilities participate. Services can only be provided in a setting other than a natural environment when early intervention cannot be achieved satisfactorily in a natural environment.

Who provides services within Babies Can't Wait?

Services are provided by agencies and individuals from both public and private sectors.

Who is eligible for Babies Can't Wait?

BCW serves Georgia children from birth up to their third birthday, regardless of income, who meet one of the following criteria:

1. Have a diagnosed physical or mental condition which is known to result in a developmental delay, such as blindness, Down syndrome, or spina bifida; or

2. Have a diagnosed developmental delay confirmed by a qualified team of professionals.

You may view the complete list of diagnoses that result in automatic eligibility for Babies Can't Wait to determine if a specific diagnosis is covered. Information about specific diagnoses may be obtained through the American Academy of Pediatrics, the National Center on Birth Defects and Developmental Disabilities at the Centers for Disease Control, and the National Organization for Rare Disorders (NORD).

HOW TO APPLY:

To apply for services you may:

1. Complete and submit the Children 1st Screening and Referral Form to the local Babies Can't Wait office that serves the county in which the child and family reside. Contact the local Babies Can't Wait office for more information.

How to contact Babies Can't Wait:

1. You may use the Children With Special Needs Coordinator locator for contact information for your local Babies Can't Wait program.
2. Babies Can't Wait has a statewide directory of information managed by Parent-to-Parent, Inc. of Georgia. The directory provides information about the BCW program located nearest to the child and family. To access the directory, call 800-229-2038 or 770-451-5484 in Atlanta.
3. The State Babies Can't Wait office number is 404-657-2850 or toll free: 888-651-8224.

Contact Information

Statewide Directory:
Parent 2 Parent of Georgia
800-229-2038
770-451-5484 (Atlanta)

State Office:
Babies Can't Wait
2 Peachtree Street, NW
11th Floor
Atlanta, GA 30303
404-657-2850
888-651-8224

ASSISTANCE PROGRAMS SERVICES

Circles of Troup County Office Parks and Rec Center
1220 Lafayette Parkway LaGrange, GA 30241 (706) 883-1687 http://circlesoftroup.org/.
Circles of Troup County is a nationally recognized program that is a high-impact approach to addressing poverty. They combine best practices in several disciplines including community organizing, case management, SMART goal setting, financial literacy, peer-to-peer counseling and learning, and child/youth development. Participants in Circles must apply and go through an interview process, and once accepted attend a 12-week class that includes a wide variety of concepts including goal setting, financial literacy, "hidden rules" of economic class and more. When they have completed the classes, the graduates are matched with two to four middle-class volunteers who commit to working with them to reach their goals. Participants are the "circle leaders" of this small group, and volunteers are "allies." The group meets on Thursdays, and other volunteers provide free meals and free childcare. The weekly classes include education meetings among the matched circles and Circles planning sessions. Meetings on the first, second, and fourth Thursdays of every month are open to visitors who are considering participating or volunteering with Circles or who want to know more about what they do.

Circles of Troup County
Thursday Meetings, Troup Baptist Association 1301 Washington Street LaGrange, GA 30240 (706) 883-1687 http://circlesoftroup.org/contact-us/. Circles of Troup County meets every Thursday at 5:30, which includes a free meal from 6:15 to 7:45 PM. Meetings on the first, second, and fourth Thursdays of every month are open to visitors who are considering participating or volunteering with Circles or who want to know more about what they do.

Emmaus Women's Shelter
321 Greenville Street LaGrange, GA 30241 (706) 883-7471 http://www.emmausshelter.com/.
Emmaus Women's Shelter provides services and assistance such as emergency shelter, food, housing, counseling, and job training.

Georgia Food Stamp Program
Supplemental Nutrition Assistance Program (SNAP) Troup County DFCS Office
1220 Hogansville Road LaGrange, GA 30241 (877) 423-4746 http://dfcs.dhs.georgia.gov/food-stamps. SNAP is a federally funded program that provides monthly benefits to low-income households to help pay for the cost of food. A household may be one person living alone, a family,

Appendix

or several unrelated individuals living together who routinely purchase and prepare meals together.

Heard County Women, Infant and Children Nutrition Center
1191 Franklin Parkway Franklin, GA 30217 (706) 298-6080 http://www.district4health.org/wic/wic-clinic-locations/. The Women, Infant and Children Nutrition Center program helps to provide low-income pregnant, postpartum, and breastfeeding women, infants, and children up to age five with nutritious food to supplement diets. They also provide information on healthy eating, breastfeeding promotion, and support and referrals to healthcare.

Highland Baptist Church Food Bank
409 Askew Avenue Hogansville, GA 30230 (706) 637-4217
Church food pantry. Please contact Pastor Terry Rainwater for more information.

Hogansville Empty Stocking Fund
Administered by the Hogansville Pilot Club Hogansville, GA 30230 https://www.facebook.com/Pilot-Club-of-Hogansville-301761163338655/info/?tab=page_info
This project, sponsored by the Hogansville Pilot Club, buys toys and clothes for needy children in the Hogansville area at Christmas.

LaGrange Personal Aid Association
416 Pierce Street LaGrange, GA 30240 (706) 882-9291 http://www.lpaa.org/
LaGrange Personal Aid Association provides a variety of programs, including LaGrange Personal Aid, which provides emergency assistance whether from disaster or illness by helping with rental, mortgage, and utility payments if the main income earner is hospitalized or out of work and seeing a doctor. The Interfaith Food Closet provides temporary and emergency food assistance to those who have proof of need. The LaGrange Empty Stocking Fund provides Christmas gifts for needy children from birth to ten years of age.

LaGrange Personal Aid Association Empty Stocking Fund
416 Pierce Street LaGrange, GA 30240 (706) 882-9291 http://www.lpaa.org/
The LaGrange Empty Stocking Fund provides Christmas gifts for needy children from birth to ten years of age.

LaGrange Personal Aid Association Interfaith Food Closet
416 Pierce Street LaGrange, GA 30240 (706) 882-9291 http://www.lpaa.org/
The Interfaith Food Closet is administered in coordination with local churches. This program provides temporary and emergency food assistance to those who have proof of need until government aid is required or medical/work circumstances change.

Meriwether County Women, Infant and Children Nutrition Center
51 Gay Connector Greenville, GA 30222 (706) 298-6080 http://www.district4health.org/wic/wic-clinic-locations/. The Women, Infant and Children Nutrition Center program helps to provide low-income pregnant, postpartum, and breastfeeding women, infants, and children up to age five with nutritious food to supplement diets. They also provide information on healthy eating, breastfeeding promotion, and support and referrals to healthcare.

Saint Peter's Catholic Church St. Vincent De Paul
200 Lafayette Parkway LaGrange, GA 30240
(706) 884-0076 www.stpeterslagrange.net
Through the St. Vincent de Paul Society, this ministry provides food and clothing to those less fortunate in the community.

Salvation Army
LaGrange Corps 202 Church Street LaGrange, GA 30240 (706) 845-0197 http://salvationarmygeorgia.org/lagrange/. The Salvation Army LaGrange on a day-to-day basis provides families in crisis situations assistance in the form of clothing, food, furniture, medical prescriptions, rent, and utilities. During the summer the organization provides a weeklong camping experience in the north Georgia Mountains to underprivileged youths. At Christmas the organization provides new clothing, new toys, and wholesome food boxes to low-income families who otherwise could not afford these items for Christmas. All requests for assistance are evaluated through a formal interview process.

Troup County Department of Family & Children Services
1220 Hogansville Road LaGrange, GA 30240 (770) 830-2178. To report child abuse CPS intake center (855) 422-4453 http://dfcs.dhs.georgia.gov/troup-county-dfcs-office.
Troup County Department of Family & Children Services investigates child abuse, finds foster homes for abused or neglected children, assists with childcare costs, job training, and other support services for low-income parents and children.

Troup County Women, Infant and Children Nutrition Center
900 Dallis Street. LaGrange, GA 30240 (706) 845-4035 http://www.district4health.org/wic/wic-clinic-locations/. The Women, Infant and Children Nutrition Center program helps to provide low-income pregnant, postpartum, and breastfeeding women, infants, and children up to age five with nutritious food to supplement diets. They also provide information on healthy eating, breastfeeding promotion, and support and referrals to healthcare.

Unity Baptist Church
Food Closet Ministry 715 South Greenwood Street LaGrange, GA 30240 (706) 882-7714 http://www.ubclagrange.org/about-.html.

Appendix

West Point Food Closet
Located in West Point Gym Highway 29 West Point, GA 31833 (770) 773-6262

STATE LICENSED CHILD CARE SERVICES IN TROUP COUNTY

Bright From the Start
(877) 255-4254 www.decal.ga.gov/#1
Bright from the Start administers the nationally recognized Georgia's Pre-K Program, licenses child care centers and home-based child care, administers federal nutrition programs, and manages voluntary quality enhancement programs. This is a website-driven child care resource for parents to visit to see what statewide programs Bright from the Start administers.

Child Care Resource & Referral
2429 Gillionville Road Albany, GA 31707 (866) 833-3552 www.ccrr.darton.edu
Child Care Resource and Referral gives referrals to child care programs to parents located in West Central Georgia and provides information to parents on how to evaluate quality child care and also about financial assistance available in meeting their child care needs.

CAFI LaGrange
104 McGregor Street LaGrange, GA 30240 (706) 882-6725 www.decal.ga.gov/#1
Serves ages infant through school age children, as well as Pre-K only. CAFI LaGrange accepts subsidies and offers the following services: transportation to and from home and school and Child and Adult Care Food Program (CACFP) and Summer Food Service Program (SFSP). License Number: CCLC-3403. Child Care Licensed Capacity: 285.

Caring and Sharing Learning Center
105 Mimosa Terrace LaGrange, GA 30241 (706) 443-6787 www.decal.ga.gov/#1
Serves ages infant through school age children. Caring and Sharing Learning Center accepts subsidies and provides the following services: drop-in care, night care, and summer care. License Number: CCLC-37103 Child Care Licensed Capacity: 27

Childcare Network #107
41 North Cary Street LaGrange, GA 30240 (706) 298-0089 www.decal.ga.gov/#1
Serves ages infant through school age children, as well as Pre-K only. Childcare Network #107 accepts subsidies and offers the following services: drop-in care, transportation to and from school, summer care, and CACFP/SFSP. License Number: CCLC-2203 Child Care Licensed Capacity: 141

Childcare Network #119
3009 West Point Road LaGrange, GA 30240 (706) 882-2025 www.decal.ga.gov/#1

Serves ages infant through school age children, as well as Pre-K only. Childcare Network #119 accepts subsidies and offers the following services: drop-in care, transportation to and from school, summer care, and CACFP/SFSP. License Number: CCLC-1456. Child Care Licensed Capacity: 130

Childcare Network #239
2001 Kia Boulevard West Point, GA 31833 (706) 408-6076 www.decal.ga.gov/#1
Serves ages infant through school age children. Childcare Network #239 accepts subsidies and offers the following services: drop-in care, night care, transportation to and from school, and CACFP/SFSP. License Number: CCLC-37305. Child Care Licensed Capacity: 155

First Baptist Child Development
100 Broad Street LaGrange, GA 30240 (706) 884-2437 www.decal.ga.gov/#1
Serves ages infant through Preschool (ages 3-4 years). First Baptist Child Development accepts subsidies. License Number: CCLC-1890. Child Care Licensed Capacity: 132

First Presbyterian Child Care
120 Broad Street LaGrange, GA 30240 (706) 884-2068 www.decal.ga.gov/#1
Serves ages infant through Preschool (ages 3-4 years). First Presbyterian Child Care accepts subsidies and offers CACFP/SFSP. License Number: CCLC-1812. Child Care Licensed Capacity: 64

God's Tomorrow
916 Colquitt Street LaGrange, GA 30241 (706) 416-1450 www.decal.ga.gov/#1
Serves ages infant through school age children. God's Tomorrow accepts subsidies and provides the following services: drop-in care, night care, transportation to and from school, summer care, and CACFP/SFSP. License Number: CCLC-4231 Child Care Licensed Capacity: 48

Happy Days Childcare Learning Center
109 Bridgewood Drive LaGrange, GA 30240 (706) 298-7390 www.decal.ga.gov/#1
Serves ages infant through school age children. Happy Days Childcare Learning Center accepts subsidies and offers the following services: drop-in care, night care, and summer care. License Number: CCLC-36455 Child Care Licensed Capacity: 96

Harper, Alma J
203 Eichelberger Drive LaGrange, GA 30241 (706) 884-6777 www.decal.ga.gov/#1
Serves ages infant through Preschool (ages 3-4). Alma J. Harper accepts subsidies and provides drop-in care. License Number: FR-0001410670. Child Care Licensed Capacity: 6

Joyful Hearts Learning Center
1402 Dogwood Circle West Point, GA 31833 (706) 412-0481 www.decal.ga.gov/#1
Serves ages infant through school age children. Joyful Hearts Learning Center does not accept

Appendix

subsidies but does provide the following services: drop-in care, night care, and summer care. License Number: CCLC-29570 Child Care Licensed Capacity: 45

Kids R Us Learning Academy
74 Youngs Mill Road LaGrange, GA 30241 (706) 668-6456
Serves ages infant to school age children. This provider also participates in subsidized child care programs. Provides drop-in and evening care. License Number: CCLC-39129. Child Care Licensed Capacity: 77

Kids First Learning Center
74 Youngs Mill Road LaGrange, GA 30241 (706) 883-6262 www.decal.ga.gov/#1
Serves ages infant through school age children. Kids First Learning Center accepts subsidies and offers the following services: drop-in care, night care, summer care, and CACFP/SFSP. License Number: CCLC-3483 Child Care Licensed Capacity: 77

Lafayette Christian School Early Learning Center
1904 Hamilton Road LaGrange, GA 30241 (706) 884-6684 www.decal.ga.gov/#1
Serves ages infant through school age children. Lafayette Christian School Early Learning Center accepts subsidies and offers CACFP/SFSP. License Number: CCLC-24175. Child Care Licensed Capacity: 482

Logan, Polly A
5096 West Point Road LaGrange, GA 30240 (706) 882-3675 www.decal.ga.gov/#1
Serves ages infant through Preschool (ages 3-4). Polly A. Logan accepts subsidies and provides summer care. License Number: FR-000002763. Child Care Licensed Capacity: 6

Maidee Smith Early Care and Learning Center
607 Union Street LaGrange, GA 30241 (706) 882-2012 www.decal.ga.gov/#1
Serves ages infant through Preschool (ages 3-4). Maidee Smith Early Care and Learning Center accepts subsidies and provides drop-in care. License Number: CCLC-1991. Child Care Licensed Capacity: 55

Mrs. Rhonda's Stay 'N Play
2767 Roanoke Road LaGrange, GA 30240 (706) 812-9494 www.decal.ga.gov/#1
Serves ages infant through school age children. Mrs. Rhonda's Stay 'N Play accepts subsidies and offers summer care and CACFP/SFSP. License Number: CCLC-9090. Child Care Licensed Capacity: 41

Pride and Joy Day Care Center
102 Durand Road LaGrange, GA 30241 (706) 812-8393 www.decal.ga.gov/#1
Serves ages infant through school age children, as well as Pre-K Only. Pride and Joy Day Care

Center accepts subsidies and offers drop-in care, summer care, and CACFP/SFSP. License Number: CCLC-308 Child-Care Licensed Capacity: 125

Robinson, Linda J
201 Lee Street Hogansville, GA 30230 (706) 637-8900 www.decal.ga.gov/#1
Serves ages infant through school age children. Linda J. Robinson accepts subsidies and provides drop-in care, night care, and summer care. License Number: FR-000006914. Child Care Licensed Capacity: 6

Rutledge, Linda J
1086 Cannonville Road LaGrange, GA 30240 (706) 884-3168 www.decal.ga.gov/#1
Serves ages infant through school age children. Linda J. Rutledge accepts subsidies and provides drop-in care, night care, and summer care. License Number: FR-9105100985. Child Care Licensed Capacity: 6

Sledge, Kimberly D
71 Willowood Road LaGrange, GA 30241 (706) 882-2775 www.decal.ga.gov/#1
Serves ages infant through school age children. Kimberly D. Sledge does not accept subsidies but does provide summer care. License Number: FR-000001549. Child Care Licensed Capacity: 6

Sledge, Sandra L
221 Beechwood Circle LaGrange, GA 30240 (706) 884-3003 www.decal.ga.gov/#1
Serves ages infant through Preschool (3-4 years). Sandra L. Sledge does not accept subsidies but does provide summer care. License Number: FR-000010058. Child Care Licensed Capacity: 6

Susan's Early Learning Center
2868 Whitesville Road LaGrange, GA 30240 (706) 845-8556 www.decal.ga.gov/#1
Serves ages infant through school age children, as well as Pre-K only. Susan's Early Learning Center accepts subsidies and offers drop-in care. License Number: CCLC-3316. Child Care Licensed Capacity: 100

Teachable Moments
1411 D Hogansville Road LaGrange, GA 30240 (706) 884-3304 www.decal.ga.gov/#1
Serves ages infant through school age children. Teachable Moments accepts subsidies. License Number: CCLC-33849. Child Care Licensed Capacity: 33

Teaching, Loving, Caring
411 E. Depot Street LaGrange, GA 30241 (706) 885-1681 www.decal.ga.gov/#1
Serves ages infant through school age children, as well as Pre-K only. Teaching, Loving, Caring accepts subsidies and provides drop-in care, summer care, and CACFP/SFSP. License Number: CCLC-529. Child Care Licensed Capacity: 170

Appendix

Thompson, Laiton K
709 Glenn Robertson Drive LaGrange, GA 30241 (706) 882-9267 www.decal.ga.gov/#1
Serves ages infant through school age children and accepts subsidies. License Number: FR-29171. Child Care Licensed Capacity: 6

Tiny Treasures Learning Center
811 Hammett Road LaGrange, GA 30241 (706) 882-1496 www.decal.ga.gov/#1
Serves ages infant through school age children, as well as Pre-K only. Tiny Treasures Learning Center accepts subsidies and offers drop-in care, transportation to and from home, night care, transportation to and from school, summer care, and CACFP/SFSP. License Number: CCLC-33127 Child Care Licensed Capacity: 120

West End Center
301 Pine Street Hogansville, GA 30230 (706) 637-0401 www.decal.ga.gov/#1
Serves ages infant through school age children. The West End Center accepts subsidies and provides the following services: drop-in care, summer care, and CACFP/SFSP. License Number: CCLC-12012 Child Care Licensed Capacity: 121

Wright, Sandy K
420 Ginger Circle LaGrange, GA 30240 (706) 845-7483 www.decal.ga.gov/#1
Serves ages infant through Preschool (3-4 years). Sandy K. Wright accepts subsidies and offers drop-in care and night care. License Number: FR-23150. Child Care Licensed Capacity: 6

Yvette's Little World Day Care Center
105 Fannin Street LaGrange, GA 30240 (706) 884-2901 www.decal.ga.gov/#1
Serves ages infant through school age children, as well as Pre-K only. Yvette's Little World Day Care Center accepts subsidies and provides drop-in care, summer care, and CACFP/SFSP. License Number: CCLC-256. Child Care Licensed Capacity: 162

Daycare Resource Connection
www.daycareresource.com
The Daycare Resource Connection is a daycare listing resource site and does not endorse, license, nor otherwise recommend listings found at The Daycare Resource Connection. They are not affiliated with any government, state, or county agencies. They suggest you check your state and local regulations or daycare licensing agency before enrolling your child in a center or home daycare.

Department of Family and Children Services—Troup County
1220 Hogansville Road LaGrange, GA 30241 (706) 298-7100 www.compass.ga.gov
The Department of Family & Children Services helps low-income and out-of-work parents get back on their feet. They can provide support services and referrals to Medicaid, food stamps and child care assistance. They are also responsible for investigating reports of child abuse.

COMMUNITY RESOURCE LISTING PROGRAMS FOR CHILDREN

Babies Can't Wait
301 Main Street LaGrange, GA 30240 (706) 845-4035 http://www.district4health.org/programs/child-health/childrens-programs/
Babies Can't Wait is a mandated program under the IDEA (Individuals with Disabilities Education Act) that is for children three and younger and their families who have disabilities or significant delays in their development. They provide evaluations, assessments, and services at no cost to their families.

Boy Scouts of America, Chattahoochee Council
1237 1st Avenue Columbus, GA 31901 (706) 327-2634 http://www.chattahoochee-bsa.org/
Boy Scouts of America, Chattahoochee Council provides support to local Scouting programs in 15 counties in Alabama and Georgia. More than 5,000 youths are members of these programs, and the programs are utilized by more than 150 local community organizations. Offers various programs for young people that encourage character building, good ethical decision making, and personal and mental fitness. Cub Scouting is for ages 7-11. Boy Scouting is for boys ages 11-17. Exploring is for both young men and women ages 14-20. Throughout the year, special events for each of these programs are put on locally including Camp Cow Pie, Boy Scout Summer Camp, and Explorer Ski Weekend.

Boys & Girls Clubs of West Georgia & Chambers County LaGrange Club
115 West Cannon Street, LaGrange, GA 30240 (706) 812-9698 http://begreatwestgeorgia.org/
Through the programs offered daily at Boys & Girls Clubs of West Georgia & Chambers County, we seek to inspire and enable all young people, especially those that need us most, to realize their full potential as responsible, productive, and caring citizens. We seek to accomplish this mission through our youth development strategy, which instills in each member the senses of belonging, usefulness, influence, and competence. Further, to ensure we reach those who need us most, we offer our programming at a very affordable rate and never turn a child away for the family's inability to pay.

Camp Academia, Inc.
1507 Vernon Road, LaGrange, GA 30240. (706) 884-4492 http://www.campacademia.com/index.html. Camp Academia, Inc. is an educational firm that targets learning disorders with the latest technology, which includes their patented Brainjogging computer software.

Camp Dogwood Grief Support Camp West Georgia Hospice
1510 Vernon Road LaGrange, GA 30241 (706) 845-3905 http://www.wghealth.org/resources/camp-dogwood/. Camp Dogwood Grief Support Camp is held each summer. Camp Dogwood is a free, three-day overnight grief support camp for children in kindergarten through eighth grade from Troup, Coweta, Heard, Meriwether, and Harris counties who have experienced the loss of

a loved one. Created in 1997 as an outreach of West Georgia Hospice, it now serves 60 children each summer. It is held at Pineland Sheriff's Camp and through art, games, and stories helps campers discover healthy ways to deal with grief and find positive ways to remember their loved one.

Camp Viola
208 Camp Viola Road LaGrange, GA 30241 (706) 298-5050 http://campviola.org/
Camp Viola provides week-long, overnight and day camp opportunities for 8-12 year olds at no cost to their families to give them an opportunity to enjoy the outdoors in a Christian setting. The camp consists of 180 acres of land near Mountville. Activities include arts and crafts and sports and recreation.

CASA of Troup and Heard Counties, Inc.
118 Ridley Avenue LaGrange, GA 30240 (706) 845-8323 http://casatroupheard.org/
CASA of Troup and Heard Counties advocate for the best interests of abused and neglected children within the court system. Our belief is that every child is entitled to a safe, stable, and permanent home. We provide screened, trained, and supervised volunteers who speak for the needs of these children, one child at a time. CASA works in collaboration with key agencies, a guardian ad litem, and community resources to achieve the child's best interests. CASA ensures that deprived children have a choice in court.

Certified Literate Community Program (CLCP)
1 College Circle, LaGrange, GA 30240 (706) 756-4645 http://www.troupclcp.org/
Certified Literate Community Program promotes community-wide literacy and encourages a love of reading, promoting literacy awareness and programs to assist students in need of basic literacy education.

Children's Advocacy Center of Troup County
701 Lincoln Street LaGrange, GA 30241 (706) 298-5064 http://www.twincedars.org/program/childrens-advocacy-troup-county/. The Children's Advocacy Center of Troup County makes sure all interviews with trauma victims are done by a trained forensic interviewer to help avoid more trauma to the victim and make sure they do not have to go through multiple interviews. They also provide trauma therapy and link victims to community-based resources to help them recover.

Circle of Care
99 Johnson Street, Building C, LaGrange, GA 30241. (706) 298-2148 ext. 1225 http://www.twincedars.org/program/circle-of-care/. Twin Cedars Circle of Care's services include home and Center Based Parent Education for adolescents ages 10-23 in Troup, Meriwether, and Heard counties.

Communities In Schools of Georgia
1220 Hogansville Road LaGrange, GA 30241 (706) 298-7121 http://www.cistroup.org/ http://www.cisga.org/. Communities in Schools promotes life success by working with youths most susceptible to school dropout; within the school setting, program addresses critical issues such as school academics, attendance, literacy, job preparedness, teen pregnancy, drug and alcohol prevention, low self-esteem, disruptive and violent behavior. Volunteers support CIS program by serving as mentors and tutors. This special connection allows students to experience a meaningful, one-on-one relationship with a caring adult.

Court Appointed Special Advocates (CASA) of Troup and Heard Counties, Inc.
118 Ridley Ave. LaGrange, GA 30240, (706) 845-8323 http://casatroupheard.org/
Volunteers gather information used to help the courts decide what is in the child's best interests to make sure they are safe and no longer victims of abuse or neglect.

First Choice Women's Center of LaGrange, Georgia
300 Harwell Avenue LaGrange, GA 30240 (706) 884-3833. (800) 395-4357 http://www.lagrangepregnancy.com/. First Choice Women's Center of LaGrange, Georgia provides confidential services and counselors for pregnancy, abortion, STDs, and other issues. These services are free of charge. Pregnancy tests, limited ultrasounds, abortion recovery support, and STD/STI information is also available.

Girl Power & Emerging Women
2170 West Point Road LaGrange, GA 30240 (706) 882-0950
Girl Power & Emerging Women inspires girls to be strong, smart, and bold. We offer programs that empower girls to embrace their value and potential, equip girls with the tools for leadership roles and community action, and prepare girls to lead successful lives.

Girl Scouts of Greater Atlanta
5601 North Allen Road SE Mableton, GA 30126 (800) 771-1139 http://www.girlscoutsatl.org/
Girl Scouts provides a fun, accepting, and nurturing environment where girls make new friends, develop a plan for their lives, and acquire the self-esteem, leadership, and life skills that are critical to their future. Our programs support Georgia Performance Standards in education and promote Leadership Development, the Arts, Healthy Life Skills, Financial Literacy, STEM (Science, Technology, Engineering, and Math), Environmental Stewardship, and Community Engagement. Girl Scouting builds girls of courage, confidence, and character, who make the world a better place.

Good Shepherd Therapeutic Center of Georgia Children's Homes and Family Ministries
Bar Rest Ranch
Warm Springs, GA 31830 (770) 567-8987 (706) 975-0236

State-licensed emergency shelter for children needing crisis assistance, assessment, and short-term housing. Also provides long-term residential and treatment for abused, neglected, and problem adolescent males who are moderately emotionally disturbed. State licensed to serve maximum of 24 children ages 6-17 years with placement priority given to Troup and Meriwether counties. The center offers therapeutic horseback riding, hippotherapy, therapeutic vaulting, wildlife rehabilitation programs, pet therapy, and a sensory integration program for public school special educational classes.

Mike Daniel Recreation Center
1220 Lafayette Parkway LaGrange, GA 30241 (706) 883-1670 http://www.trouprec.org/programs.html. The Mike Daniel Recreation Center and Troup County Parks and Recreation offer many fitness and recreational programs for all ages. They have athletic leagues that include co-ed, girls, boys, and adult basketball, indoor soccer, and floor hockey. Classes offered include karate, ballet, dance, senior hydrobics, tennis, POUND, Zumba, Pilates, and functional training.

Salvation Army
LaGrange Corps 202 Church Street LaGrange, GA 30240 (706) 845-0197 http://salvationarmygeorgia.org/lagrange/. During the summer the organization provides a weeklong camping experience in the north Georgia Mountains to underprivileged youths. All requests for assistance are evaluated through a formal interview process.

Troup County Health Department
900 Dallis Street, Suite A LaGrange, GA 30240 (706) 845-4085 http://www.district4health.org/clinic-sites/troup-county/. The Troup County Health Department offers many programs and services such as Children 1st, Babies Can't Wait, WIC, teen services, and many other healthcare services as well.

CHILDREN'S HEALTH SERVICES

Children 1st
District 4 Health Department
301 Main Street
LaGrange, GA 30240
(706) 845-4035 http://www.district4health.org/programs/child-health/childrens-programs/
Children 1st program of the District 4 Health Department connects parents and children up to age five with medical preventative care or developmental services. Some of these include well-baby checkups, immunizations, and WIC referrals.

Children's Medical Services District 4 Health Department
301 Main Street
LaGrange, GA 30240
(706) 845-4035 http://www.district4health.org/programs/child-health/childrens-programs/
Children's Medical Services District 4 Health Department provides healthcare for children and youths from birth to age 21 who have eligible chronic medical conditions.

Kid Station Pediatrics
301 Medical Drive
Suite 504
LaGrange, GA 30240
(706) 882-5437 http://www.wgphysicians.org
West Georgia Physicians' Kid Station Pediatrics provides pediatric care for newborns through adolescents. Drs. Kalyani Rajeev and Torey Harden provide an array of services including checkups, newborn care, immunizations, adolescent medicine, and asthma management, among others.

LaGrange Pediatrics
1527 Vernon Road
LaGrange, GA 30240
(706) 883-6363 http://www.lagrangepediatrics.com/
Dr. Suzie Schuessler is licensed in both Georgia and Alabama and offers care for children of all ages. Services provided include checkups, newborn care, adolescent medicine, immunizations, allergy injections, asthma management, and filling out forms for schools as needed.

LaGrange Personal Aid Association
416 Pierce Street
LaGrange, GA 30240
(706) 882-9291 http://www.lpaa.org/
LaGrange Personal Aid Association can help with prescription fill and refill payments and help with the purchase of medically related items.

Pediatric Associates of LaGrange, PC
205 Calumet Center Road
LaGrange, GA 30241
(706) 885-1961 http://www.pediatricsoflagrange.com/
Dr. Lisa Allardice of Pediatric Associates of LaGrange, PC offers medical care from birth through adolescence. Dr. Allardice and her team provide a full range of diagnostic and preventative health care. Pediatricians on staff include Drs. Karyn Hunnicutt, George Lechacz, Lacy Tumambing, and Eric Zerla.

Appendix

The Children's Clinic, LLC
1550 Doctors Drive
LaGrange, GA 30240
(706) 884-2686 http://childrenscliniclc.com/
The Children's Clinic, LLC provides care for children of all ages from newborns to adolescents. Offers same-day sick visits and urgent care on weekends, holidays, and evenings.

Troup County Health Department
900 Dallis Street
Suite A
LaGrange, GA 30240
(706) 845-4085 http://troupcohealth.org/child-health/
The Troup County Health Department offers many services for the well-being of children in the area. These include Health Checks, the Safe Kids Program, Children First, immunizations, and health screenings. Health Checks is a program for children from birth to age 21 who are Medicaid/Non Medicaid recipients, with a special emphasis on high-risk infants. They offer comprehensive physical exams including developmental and nutritional assessments.

Twin Cedars Youth and Family Services
1022 E Depot Street
LaGrange, GA 30241
(706) 884-1717 https://www.twincedars.org
Twin Cedars Youth and Family Services, Inc. provides residential and community-based services in LaGrange, Macon, Columbus, and East Alabama. Connecting with our communities, Twin Cedars provides a wide range of programs, in order to meet individual community need. Our programs are very diverse, from prevention to advocacy, to maximum oversight residential programs. Please browse our website to learn more about each of our programs.

COMMUNITY FAMILY ASSISTANCE SERVICES

LaGrange Personal Aid Association
416 Pierce Street
LaGrange, GA 30240
(706) 882-9291 http://www.lpaa.org/
The LaGrange Personal Aid Association offers a variety of programs including LaGrange Personal Aid, which provides emergency assistance whether from disaster or illness by helping with rental, mortgage, and utility payments if the main income earner is hospitalized or out of work and seeing a doctor. The Interfaith Food Closet provides temporary and emergency food assistance to those who have proof of need. The LaGrange Empty Stocking Fund provides Christmas gifts for needy children from birth to ten years of age.

Saint Vincent De Paul Society Outreach
200 Lafayette Parkway
LaGrange, GA 30240
(706) 884-0076 http://www.stpeterslagrange.net/ministries/svdp/
The Saint Vincent De Paul Society Outreach program is based out of St. Peter's Catholic church and provides access to thrift stores, food pantries, temporary housing, emergency shelter, medical care and prescription assistance (crisis situations), assistance with utilities, and more.

Salvation Army
LaGrange Corps
202 Church Street
LaGrange, GA 30240
(706) 845-0197 http://salvationarmygeorgia.org/lagrange/
The Salvation Army LaGrange on a day-to-day basis provides to families in crisis situations assistance in the form of clothing, food, furniture, medical prescriptions, rent, and utilities. During the summer the organization provides a weeklong camping experience in the north Georgia Mountains to underprivileged youths. At Christmas the organization provides new clothing, new toys, and wholesome food boxes to low-income families who otherwise would not be able to afford these items for Christmas. All requests for assistance are evaluated through a formal interview process.

State Court Public Defender
100 Ridley Avenue
Suite 3400
LaGrange, GA 30240
(706) 883-2170
http://www.troupcountyga.org/public_defender%20State%20and%20Superior.html
State Court public defenders can be appointed by the court or can represent those who cannot afford representation in court.

COMMUNITY FOOD BANK RESOURCES

Baptist Tabernacle
849 South Davis Road LaGrange, GA 30241
(706) 882-0087 www.baptisttabernacle.ws
The Baptist Tabernacle provides the following ministries to the LaGrange community: food closet, clothes closet, puppet, homefolks, care, and HUB student, along with Hunters for Christ, Brotherhood, Children's Church, God's Helping Hands, Lighthouse Keepers, F.L.O.C.K., Sunday School, Vacation Bible School, Rock Middle School Students, Faithriders, Radio Ministry, Conquering Chemical Dependency, Churches Helping Churches, and Media Ministry.
Food closet hours: Thursdays, 9:00am

Appendix

Christian Service Center, Inc.
5342 Cusseta Road Lanett, AL 36863 (334) 576-3552 www.christianservicecenter.homestead.com The purpose of the Christian Service Center is to provide food, clothing, household and personal items, along with other services to the less fortunate in our community. Hours: Mondays and Thursdays, 9:00am-Noon

Feeding the Valley Food Bank LaGrange Location
118 Gordon Commercial Drive LaGrange, GA 30240
(762) 822-1712
http://www.feedingthevalley.org/plaintext/aboutus/ab outus.aspx
Feeding the Valley Food Bank serves as a center for the reception and distribution of donated food and grocery products. They pick up and receive truckloads of food and grocery products from national and local retail donors. In addition, area businesses, individuals, civic groups, schools, and churches conduct food drives throughout the year to provide food for our programs. They collaborate with member partner agencies that receive food from our warehouse and then distribute to families in need within their neighborhoods. Because of our large area of service, these agencies are a vital outreach to families in need. They have warehouse locations in both Columbus and LaGrange.

First Baptist Church Food Closet
301 East Eighth Street West Point, GA 31833 (706) 645-2969 www.fbcwestpoint.com
In collaboration with the First United Methodist Church of West Point, First Baptist Church Food Closet is an outreach ministry for residents of West Point, providing a food closet as well as emergency help for the community.
Hours: Wednesdays, 9:30am-Noon

First United Methodist Church
401 Broad Street LaGrange, GA 30241 (706) 884-4635 http://www.lagrangefumc.org/
First United Methodist of LaGrange provides local outreach in the form of Meals on Wheels, Soup Kitchen, and Community Care.
Soup Kitchen Hours: Mondays and Wednesdays, 11:30am-Noon
Community Care Hours: Tuesdays and Thursdays, 9:00am-11:00am

First United Methodist Church of West Point
306 East Seventh Street West Point, GA 31833 (706) 645-1379 www.westpointfumc.org
The First United Method Church of West Point offers the following services: West Point Food Closet (in collaboration with the First Baptist Church), Meals on Wheels, Soup Kitchen, Local Mission Projects, Habitat for Humanity, Chattahoochee Fuller Center Project, West Point Elementary Clothes Closet, Heartline Ministry, and CIA (senior transportation).
Food Closet Hours: Wednesdays, 9:30am-Noon
Soup Kitchen Hours: Thursdays, 12:00pm-12:30pm

Highland Baptist Church Food Bank
409 Askew Avenue Hogansville, GA 30230 (706) 637-4217
Church food pantry. Please contact Pastor Terry Rainwater for more information.

Interfaith Food Closet
1810B 30th Street Valley, AL 36854 (334) 768-3663
Interfaith Food Closet offers a food bank to the community.
Hours: Monday-Friday, 8:00am-5:00pm.

LaGrange Personal Aid Association Interfaith Food Closet
416 Pierce Street LaGrange, GA 30240 (706) 882-9291 http://www.lpaa.org/
The Interfaith Food Closet is administered in coordination with local churches. This program provides temporary and emergency food assistance to those who have proof of need until government aid is required or medical/work circumstances change.

Meals on Wheels First Baptist Church on the Square
100 Broad Street LaGrange, GA 30240 (706) 884-5631 http://www.fbclagrange.org/missions/local/. Every Tuesday, from 10:00 to 11:30, teams of volunteers prepare meals and deliver them to people who are in need of a hot meal.

Meals on Wheels First United Methodist of LaGrange
401 Broad Street LaGrange, GA 30240 (706) 884-4635 http://www.lagrangefumc.org/outreach/local-outreach/. The Meals on Wheels outreach ministry at First United Methodist of LaGrange is conducted each Monday. Over 550 people are served per month through this program. The meals are cooked, assembled, and distributed in the Methodist Ministries Center kitchen area.

Meals on Wheels St. Mark's Episcopal Church
207 North Greenwood Street LaGrange, GA (706) 845-8323 http://www.stmarkslg.org/ministries/meals-on-wheels/. Volunteers prepare and deliver a hot meal to over 100 people every Wednesday, including holidays. In the summer months, parishioners donate produce from their gardens, allowing for the inclusion of fresh salads and vegetables in the weekly meal.

Saint Peter's Catholic Church St. Vincent De Paul
200 Lafayette Parkway LaGrange, GA 30240 (706) 884-0076 www.stpeterslagrange.net
Through the St. Vincent de Paul Society, this ministry provides food and clothing to those less fortunate in the community.

Salvation Army
202 Church Street LaGrange, GA 30240 (706) 884-6842 www.salvationarmygeorgia.org/lagrange. The Salvation Army provides services to every zip code in Troup County, including emergency assistance for individuals and families in a crisis situation, by ministering to their

needs in the areas of food, clothing, lodging, transportation, supplies for infants, prescription vouchers, rent and bill-payment assistance, counseling and referrals to crisis centers.

Troup County Department of Family and Children Services
1220 Hogansville Road LaGrange, GA 30241 (706) 298-7100 http://dfcs.dhs.georgia.gov/troup-county-dfcs-office. Troup County DFCS Office provides food assistance programs and food stamps, along with adoption, after-school services, child abuse and neglect, education and training, energy assistance, foster care, Medicaid, prevention and family support, refugee resettlement, subsidized child care, TeenWork, and temporary assistance for needy families. Hours: Monday-Friday, 8:00am-5:00pm

Unity Baptist Church Food Closet Ministry
715 South Greenwood Street LaGrange, GA 30240 (706) 882-7714 http://www.ubclagrange.org/about-.html

West Point Food Closet Located in West Point Gym Highway 29
West Point, GA 31833 (770) 773-6262 Food pantry.

COMMUNITY HOUSING ASSISTANCE SERVICES

Community Action for Improvement (CAFI)
1380 Lafayette Parkway LaGrange, GA 30241 (706) 884-2651 http://www.cafi-ga.org/
Community Action for Improvement provides programs for affordable housing and weatherization programs to help make homes more energy efficient. They also provide assistance with the Energy Assistance Program. Serves Heard, Meriwether, and Troup counties.

Dependable Affordable Sustainable Housing (DASH) LaGrange
1200 4th Avenue LaGrange, GA 30240 (706) 298-0221 http://www.dashlagrange.org/
DASH (Dependable Affordable Sustainable Housing) LaGrange provides homeownership opportunities, safe and affordable rental options, financial education, credit repair counseling, and home improvement loan programs.

Franklin Housing Authority
900 South River Road Franklin, GA 30217 (706) 675-6060
Franklin Housing Authority provides low-income residents with housing assistance through the management of Low Rent Public Housing. This program is income-based, and the eligibility guidelines are set by HUD. There may be waiting lists for these rentals.

Habitat for Humanity
333 Main Street LaGrange, GA 30241 (706) 837-0702 https://tcchfh.wordpress.com/.

Habitat for Humanity LaGrange helps build affordable housing for those in need; houses are sold to partner families at no profit and financed with affordable loans.

Hogansville Housing Authority
200 West Boyd Road Hogansville, GA 30230 (706) 637-8153
Hogansville Housing Authority provides low-income residents with housing assistance through the management of Low Rent Public Housing. This program is income-based, and the eligibility guidelines are set by HUD.

Housing Authority of the City of Greenville, Georgia
3041 Highway 100 Greenville, GA 30222 (706) 672-1353
The Housing Authority of the City of Greenville offers one public housing community with 80 units for families and senior/disabled individuals.

Housing Authority of the City of West Point, Georgia
1201 East 12th Street West Point, GA 31833 (706) 645-1202 http://www.columbushousing.org/page.asp?urh=PropertiesViewer&id=17. The Housing Authority of the City of West Point, Georgia, provides housing for eligible low-income families. This location has 223 housing units, two outdoor play areas, and a basketball court. Units available range from studio apartments to five-bedroom units. The units have stoves, refrigerators, and washer/dryer connections.

Housing Authority of the County of Harris County, Georgia
420 Copeland Avenue Hamilton, GA 31811 (706) 628-4266 http://www.columbushousing.org/page.asp?urh=PropertiesViewer&id=16. The Housing Authority of the County of Harris, Georgia, offers Low Rent Public Housing apartments that are located in three cities in the county: Hamilton, Pine Mountain, and Waverly Hall. There are a total of 43 units with bedroom sizes ranging from one to four.

LaGrange Housing Authority Benjamin Harvey Hill Homes
201 Chatham Street LaGrange, GA 30240. (706) 882-6416 http://www.phalagrange.net/
The Housing Authority of LaGrange provides safe rental housing for eligible low-income families, the elderly, or those with disabilities who qualify. The Benjamin Harvey Hills Homes are some of the 420 units offered and can include one-bedroom units up to four-bedroom units that also have a living area, kitchen, and bath.

LaGrange Housing Authority Lucy Morgan Homes
611 Borton Street LaGrange, GA 30240 (706) 884-9586 http://www.phalagrange.net/
The Housing Authority of LaGrange provides safe rental housing for eligible low-income families, the elderly, or those with disabilities who qualify. The Lucy Morgan Homes are some of the 420 units offered and can include one-bedroom units up to four-bedroom units that also have a living area, kitchen, and bath.

Appendix

LaGrange Personal Aid Association
416 Pierce Street LaGrange, GA 30240 (706) 882-9291 http://www.lpaa.org/
The LaGrange Personal Aid Association offers a variety of programs, including LaGrange Personal Aid, which provides emergency assistance whether from disaster or illness by helping with rental, mortgage, and utility payments if the main income earner is hospitalized or out of work and seeing a doctor.

MEDICAID ENROLLMENT SERVICES

Right from the Start Medicaid Program Heard and Troup Counties
RSM Project Office
WellStar West Georgia Medical Center 1514 Vernon Road
3rd Floor
LaGrange, GA 30240
(706) 845-4246 http://dfcs.dhs.georgia.gov/right-start-medicaid-program
The Right from the Start Medicaid (RSM) Outreach Project provides access to affordable comprehensive health care coverage to working families in Heard County.

Troup County Department of Family & Children Services
1220 Hogansville Road
LaGrange, GA 30241
(770) 830-2178
(877) 423-4746 http://dfcs.dhs.georgia.gov/medicaid
Medicaid is a program that provides health care services to individuals who meet the requirements for income, resources, and citizenship. Cooperation with Georgia Department of Human Services Division of Child Support Services is a requirement of receiving certain types of Medicaid.

COMMUNITY SHELTER RESOURCES

A Higher Calling
305 Louise Lane Griffin, GA 30223 (678) 603-2880 www.ahighercallinggriffin.org
A Higher Calling provides shelter and transitional housing for the homeless citizens in the community by having relationships with local churches, federal, state, and local governments, local businesses, health and wellness providers, educational institutions, mental health and substance abuse counselors, social service institutions, and faith-based and grass-root organizations.

American Red Cross
900 Dallis Street Suite C LaGrange, GA 30240 (706) 884-5818 http://www.redcross.org/local/georgia/locations/central-midwest. The American Red Cross exists to provide compassionate

care to those in need. Our network of generous donors, volunteers, and employees share a mission of preventing and relieving suffering, here at home and around the world, through five key service areas: disaster relief (providing shelter, food, health and mental health services), supporting America's military families (emergency communications, training, support to wounded warriors and veterans, and access to community resources), lifesaving blood (blood donation), health and safety services (CPR, first aid, and lifeguard training) and international services (responding to disasters, building safer communities, and teaching of the rules of war).

Ark Refuge Ministry (ARK)
504 East Depot Street LaGrange, GA 30241 (706) 845-0335 http://arkrefuge.net/
The Ark Refuge Ministry is a non-profit organization dedicated to the specific goal of restoring the lives of individuals and families affected by issues related to homelessness and substance abuse. The ARK has been a homeless, substance abuse center in LaGrange, Georgia, and the surrounding communities for over twenty years. They offer their residents health care sponsored by personal aid and Troup Cares, have the S.A.F.E. program (offer Support, Apparel, Food, and Emergency shelter for their residents), offer counseling services 24 hours a day and 7 days a week, have daily Bible study, assist clients in obtaining their GED, and have job training through the GA Department of Labor and The Georgia Works Program.

Community Action for Improvement, Inc. (CAFI)
1380 Lafayette Parkway LaGrange, GA 30241 (706) 884-2651 www.cafi-ga.org
CAFI has helped more than one million residents through the carefully planned administration of social services, advocacy, and community education. We empower citizens to become self-sufficient by offering programs and services that enable individuals and families to emerge from economic despair, prevent homelessness, and enhance educational goals for an improved quality of life.

Emmaus Women's Shelter
312 Greenville Street LaGrange, GA 30241 (706) 883-7471 www.emmausshelter.com
To provide refuge, restoration, and reintegration for homeless women and their families, including fathers, sons, and veterans.

Fellowship Deliverance Ministries
207 West Mulberry Street LaGrange, GA 30240 (706) 845-0071 www.fdm1.org
To provide support services and assist in the development of a moral, healthy community through the establishment of non-profit programs that aid individuals in need of assistance with daily living due to unexpected hardships such as loss of income, natural disasters, death, homelessness, etc.

Georgia Sheriffs' Youth Homes
3000 Highway 42 North Stockbridge, GA 30281 (770) 914-1076 www.georgiasheriffsyouth.org

The Georgia Sheriffs' Youth Homes was established to give our state's most at-risk children the love, safety, and stability needed to become mature, successful adults.

God's Dwelling Place
LaGrange, GA 30241 (706) 412-9004
God's Dwelling Place is a women's shelter that offers food, clothing, shelter, job search skills, and counseling.

Harmony House Domestic Violence Shelter
LaGrange, GA (706) 885-1525 www.harmonyhousega.org
Harmony House provides emergency, safe, confidential shelter to victims of domestic violence.

Hope's Inn for Single Mothers
106 North Monroe Street Lafayette, AL 36862 (334) 864-0890
Hope's Inn is a short-term crisis shelter for women and children.

LaGrange Housing Authority—Benjamin Harvey Hill Homes
201 Chatham Street LaGrange, GA 30240 (706) 882-6416 www.phalagrange.net
The Housing Authority of the City of LaGrange, GA, has been providing low-income housing to families in the Troup County area since 1953.

LaGrange Housing Authority—Lucy Morgan Homes
611 Borton Street LaGrange, GA 30240 (706) 884-9856 www.phalagrange.net
The Housing Authority of the City of LaGrange, GA, has been providing low-income housing to families in the Troup County area since 1953.

Troup County Homeless Coalition
LaGrange, GA 30240 homeless helpline: (706) 298-7228 (762) 822-1712 http://www.tchomeless.com/about.html. The Troup County Homeless Coalition is a diverse group of volunteers, homeless service provider agencies, homeless persons, advocates, and concerned citizens committed to ending homelessness through education, advocacy, and coordinated services. No homeless person or at-risk individual or family shall be without proper services when needing assistance. We also provide a forum for exchanging information between member agencies and homeless individuals.

HOTLINE NUMBERS RESOURCES

Al-Anon Family Group Headquarters, Inc.
(757) 563-1600 http://www.al-anon.alateen.org/
Al-Anon Family Group Headquarters, Inc. provides help and resources for friends and family of problem drinkers. The link above provides Al-Anon and Alateen information and meeting locations.

Alcoholics Anonymous
(404) 525-3178 http://www.aa.org/
The Alcoholics Anonymous hotline is a 24-hour hotline. You can learn about meetings and support in your area.

Alzheimer's Association
(800) 272-3900 http://www.alz.org/
The Alzheimer's Association has a 24/7 Helpline that serves people with memory loss, caregivers, health care professionals, and the public.

American Cancer Society
250 Williams Street NW Atlanta, GA 30303 (404) 315-1123
(800) 227-2345 http://www.cancer.org/index
The American Cancer Society phone line and website can help you find local support groups and other services in your area such as rides to appointments, etc.

American Lung Association
(800) 548-8252 http://www.lung.org/about-us/
The American Lung Association phone line and website provide information on lung health and diseases, how to quit smoking, and research.

Autism Society
(800) 328-8476 http://www.autism-society.org/
The Autism Society provides information and referral to many services and support across the country.

National Alcoholism and Substance Abuse Information Center
(800) 784-6776
http://www.addictioncareoptions.com/
The National Alcoholism and Substance Abuse Information Center is a comprehensive database of the leading drug and alcohol treatment centers both internationally and in the United States for every level of treatment option from affordable to luxury. Our national database is consistently updated to include all of the treatment options near you, as well as the leading addiction treatment centers in the country for those who are able to travel outside of their local area to receive the best possible care.

National Suicide Prevention Lifeline
(800) 273-8255 http://www.suicidepreventionlifeline.org/
The National Suicide Prevention Lifeline is a 24-hour, toll-free, confidential suicide prevention hotline available to anyone in suicidal crisis or emotional distress.

National Teen Dating Abuse Hotline
(866) 331-9474 http://www.loveisrespect.org/
The National Teen Dating Abuse Hotline is for anyone concerned about dating abuse, whether teenagers or parents.

Poison Control
(800) 222-1222 http://www.aapcc.org/
Poison Control Centers offer free, confidential medical advice 24 hours a day, seven days a week through the Poison Help line. This service provides a primary resource for poisoning information and helps reduce costly hospital visits through in-home treatment.

Substance Abuse and Mental Health Services Administration National Helpline
(800) 662-4357 http://www.samhsa.gov/find-help/national-helpline
The Substance Abuse and Mental Health Services Administration National Helpline is a confidential, free, 24-hour-a-day, 365-day-a-year information service, in English and Spanish, for individuals and family members facing mental health and/or substance use disorders. This service provides referrals to local treatment facilities, support groups, and community-based organizations. Callers may also order free publications and other information.

The National Domestic Violence Hotline
(800) 799-7233 or (800)787-3224 (TTY) http://www.thehotline.org/
The National Domestic Violence Hotline has highly trained advocates available 24/7 to talk confidentially with anyone experiencing domestic violence, seeking resources or information, or questioning unhealthy aspects of their relationship.

Vet2Vet Veteran's Crisis Line
(877) 838-2838 http://www.veteranscall.us/
Vet2Vet Veteran's Crisis Line is a toll-free line targeted to the population of returning armed forces men and women and veterans from previous conflicts and wars. This "life" line is a confidential connection which plans to utilize trained peer veterans ready to provide hope and help 24 hours a day, 7 days a week.

Veterans Crisis Line
(800) 273-8255 and Press 1 https://www.veteranscrisisline.net/
The Veterans Crisis Line connects veterans in crisis and their families with Department of Veterans Affairs responders 24/7. It is a confidential service. You can also text them, and chat online with someone.

Suggested Reading

The Baby Owner's Manual: Operating Instructions, Trouble-Shooting Tips, and Advice on First-Year Maintenance (Owner's and Instruction Manual) by Louis Borgenicht M.D., Joe Borgenicht

What to Expect the First Year by Heidi Murkoff and Sharon Mazel

The Happiest Baby on the Block; Fully Revised and Updated Second Edition: The New Way to Calm Crying and Help Your Newborn Baby Sleep Longer by Harvey Karp

Toddler Discipline for Every Age and Stage: Effective Strategies to Tame Tantrums, Overcome Challenges, and Help Your Child Grow by Aubrey Hargis

The Montessori Toddler: A Parent's Guide to Raising a Curious and Responsible Human Being by Simone Davies (Author), Hiyoko Imai (Illustrator)

The Ultimate Toddler Activity Guide: Fun & Educational Activities to Do with Your Toddler by Mrs. Autumn McKay

Your Two-Year-Old: Terrible or Tender by Louise Bates Ames

Your Three-Year-Old: Friend or Enemy by Louise Bates Ames and Frances L. Ilg

Your Four-Year-Old: Wild and Wonderful by Louise Bates Ames

Your Five-Year-Old: Sunny and Serene by Louise Bates Ames and Frances L. Ilg

Index

A
Activity boxes, 62
ADHD (attention deficit hyperactivity disorder), 67
Affirmations, 74–75
Alphabet
    decorating room with letters from, 56
    kindergarten readiness checklist, 91
    letter scrapbook, 88
    sculpting with Play-Doh, 89
    song, 19
American Academy of Pediatrics (AAP)
    on autism screenings, 38, 44, 53
    on screen time, 16–17, 32
Art projects
    2 years, 56
    3 years, 64
    4 years, 80
    5 years, 85, 89
    kindergarten readiness checklist, 93
Assistance programs services, 112–15
Asthma, 17
Attention deficit hyperactivity disorder (ADHD), 67
Attention-seeking behavior, 51
Attention span, 88
Autism Spectrum Disorder (ASD)
    screening for, 38, 44, 53
    screen time and, 67

B
Babies Learning on Course for Kindergarten Success (BLOCKS), 108–11
Bath time
    safety, 32
    water play, 24, 42, 64

Bedtime routines, 13, 29, 62
Behavior issues. *See also* **Discipline**
    9 to 12 months, 20
    12 to 15 months, 31
    18 to 24 months, 40
    24 to 30 months, 51, 53–54
    4 years, 73–74
    5 years, 90
    screen time and, 67
Bipolar illness, 67
Birth to 3 months, 2–5
BLOCKS (Babies Learning on Course for Kindergarten Success), 108–11
Board games, 79
Boredom, 68–69, 99
Brain development. *See also* **Cognitive milestones; Memory**
    birth to 3 months, 3–4
    birth to 3 years, i–iii
    12 months, 23–24
    cell phone radiation and, v
    love and safety, effect on, ii
    reading and, 19, 41
    screen time and, 32, 67–69
    self-control and, 29
Breastfeeding, iv–v, 32

C
Caregiver tips, 20
Cars
    child car seats, 33
    secondhand smoke and, 17
    unattended children in, 33
Cell phone distracted parenting, iv–v, 16–17, 32, 99
Cell phone radiation, v
Cell phones. *See* **Screen time**

Child care services, 115–19
Childproofing
    9 to 12 months, 20, 24
    15 months, 31, 32–33
    30 to 36 months, 58
Children's health services, 123–25
Chores
    15 to 18 months, 35
    24 to 30 months, 55
    30 to 36 months, 64
    5 years, 85, 88
    training children's brains for success and, 102
Cigarette smoke, 17
Cognitive milestones
    4 months, 8
    6 months, 10
    9 months, 14
    1 year, 21
    18 months, 37
    2 years, 43
    30 months, 53
    3 years, 60
    4 years, 76
    5 years, 86
Colic, 3
Color identification, 64, 79, 89
Communication. *See* **Language and conversation; Language/ communication milestones**
Community resources, 112–36
    assistance programs services, 112–15
    child care services, 115–19
    children's health services, 123–25
    community resource listing programs, 120–23
    family assistance services, 125–26
    food bank resources, 126–29
    hotline numbers resources, 133–35
    housing assistance services, 129–31
    Medicaid enrollment services, 131
    shelter resources, 131–33
Confidence, 24, 88, 102
Consistency
    discipline and, 51
    routines and, 101
Counting and numbers
    12 months, 23
    30 to 36 months, 62–63
    kindergarten readiness checklist, 92–93
Crawling
    3 to 6 months, 6
    6 to 9 months, 12
    9 to 12 months, 18
    12 to 15 months, 28
Creativity, 69. *See also* **Art projects**
Criticism, 64
Crying. *See also* **Tantrums**
    birth to 3 months, 2–3
    bedtimes and, 13
    colic, 3

D
Delayed gratification, 69, 98, 101–2
Depression and anxiety, 17
Developmental delays, 38, 44, 53, 67. *See also* **Milestones**
Diet. *See* **Eating and diet**
Digital media and the brain, 67–69. *See also* **Screen time**
Discipline. *See also* **Behavior issues; Patience**
    15 months, 31
    brain development and, 101
    consistency and, 51
    limits, setting, 40, 50–51, 62, 101
    potty training and, 49
    rewards vs. punishments, 20, 41, 49, 59
    rules and consequences, 31, 40, 62, 74, 101
    sexuality questions and, 73–74
    spanking, 20
    spoiling children and, ii, 2, 7
    time-outs, 20, 62
Drawing, 64
Drowning, 32
Ducanda, Anne-Lise, 67
Dunckley, Victoria, 67

Index

E
Ear infections, 17
Early intervention programs
    Babies Learning on Course for Kindergarten Success (BLOCKS), 108–11
    milestones and, 9, 15, 22, 38
Eating and diet
    breastfeeding, iv–v, 32
    food sensitivities and, 3
    healthy choices for, 32, 101
    picky eaters and, 29
    utensils and tools for, 42
Education. *See* **School readiness; Teaching tips**
18 to 24 months, 39–44
Emotional development. *See also* **Social/emotional milestones; Tantrums**
    15 to 18 months, 34
    18 to 24 months, 39, 41
    30 to 36 months, 63
    4 years, 78
    5 years, 85, 90
    cell phone distracted parenting and, iv, 16–17, 32, 99
    empathy and, 35–36
    managing feelings, 20
    self-awareness and, 35
    understanding others' feelings, 59
Empathy, 35–36
Expectations, 74

F
Face-to-face interaction, 16–17, 32
Family history, 102
Fathers. *See* **Parents**
Fears, ii, 13, 48
Fever, 4–5
Fickleness, 53
15-month-old milestones, 30
15 to 18 months, 34–38
Fine motor skills
    6 to 9 months, 12
    12 to 15 months, 28
    30 to 36 months, 58
    kindergarten readiness checklist, 92
    screen time and, 16
Firearms, 33
5-year-olds, 84–94
    kindergarten readiness checklist, 91–94
    milestones, 86–87
    teaching tips for, 88–90
Food bank resources, 126–29
Foods. *See* **Eating and diet**
4-month-old milestones, 8–9
4-year-olds, 72–80
    behavior of, 73–74
    frustration experienced by, 74–75
    milestones, 76–77
    sexuality questions and, 73
    teaching tips for, 78–80
Friends
    2 years, 56
    24 to 30 months, 48
    30 to 36 months, 58, 59
    4 years, 72
    5 years, 84
Frustrations, 73–75

G
Games. *See also* **Pretend play; Songs and nursery rhymes**
    birth to 3 months, 4
    9 to 12 months, 18
    12 to 15 months, 31
    15 to 18 months, 34
    18 to 24 months, 39, 41–42
    24 to 30 months, 48, 55–57
    30 to 36 months, 62–66
    4 years, 78–80
    5 years, 88–90
    bath time and water play, 24, 42, 64
Goodbye routines, 13, 18, 20
Grocery shopping as teaching time, 65, 79
Gross motor skills. *See* **Mobility and gross motor skills**

Grouping games, 78–79
Guns, 33

H
Health and wellness behaviors, 13, 55, 94. *See also* **Eating and diet; Safety; Screen time; Teeth**
Hickory Dickory Dock, 24
Homeless shelter resources, 131–33
Hotline numbers resources, 133–35
Housing assistance services, 129–31
Humpty Dumpty, 24

I
Illness
    in infants, 4–5
    mental, 17, 67
    secondhand smoke and, 17
    symptoms of, 5
Imagination, 56. *See also* **Art projects; Games**
Imitation, 19, 28
Independence
    12 to 15 months, 28, 32
    15 to 18 months, 32, 35
    24 to 30 months, 53
    5 years, 85
Itsy Bitsy Spider, 25

K
Kindergarten readiness checklist, 91–94

L
Language and conversation. *See also* **Vocabulary, building**
    birth to 3 months, 2, 3–4
    3 to 6 months, 6–7
    6 to 9 months, 12
    9 to 12 months, 18, 19–20
    12 to 15 months, 23, 28, 31
    15-month milestones, 30
    15 to 18 months, 34
    18 to 24 months, 39–40
    24 to 30 months, 48, 55
    30 to 36 months, 58, 59
    4 years, 72
    5 years, 85
    kindergarten readiness checklist, 91
    screen time and, 16–17
Language/communication milestones
    4 months, 8
    6 months, 10
    9 months, 14
    1 year, 21
    18 months, 37
    2 years, 43
    30 months, 52
    3 years, 60
    4 years, 76
    5 years, 86
Left handedness, 89
Limits, setting, 40, 50–51, 62, 101
Listening skills, 91
Logical thinking, 58
Love, expressing, ii, 62

M
Manners, 79, 90, 102. *See also* **Social skills**
Mary Had a Little Lamb, 25
Math, 64, 84–85, 92–93. *See also* **Counting and numbers**
Medicaid enrollment services, 131
Medical consultation. *See also* **Milestones**
    for crying, 3
    for fever, 5
Medications, 5
Memory
    9 to 12 months, 18–19
    30 to 36 months, 58, 65
    4 years, 78
    5 years, 89
    repetition and, 18

Mental illnesses, 17, 67
Milestones
    4 months, 8–9
    6 months, 10–11
    9 months, 14–15
    1 year, 21–22
    15 months, 30
    18 months, 37–38
    2 years, 43–44
    30 months, 52–54
    3 years, 60–61
    4 years, 76–77
    5 years, 86–87
Misbehaviors. *See* **Behavior issues**
Mistakes, 88, 98–100
Mobility and gross motor skills
    3 to 6 months, 6
    6 to 9 months, 12
    9 to 12 months, 18
    12 to 15 months, 28
    15-month milestones, 30
    15 to 18 months, 34
    24 to 30 months, 48
    30 to 36 months, 58
    4 years, 72
    5 years, 84
    kindergarten readiness checklist, 92
    screen time and, 16
Mothers. *See* **Parents**
Movement/physical milestones
    4 months, 8
    6 months, 10
    9 months, 14
    1 year, 22
    18 months, 37
    2 years, 43
    30 months, 52
    3 years, 61
    4 years, 77
    5 years, 87
Museums, 103–4
Music. *See also* **Songs and nursery rhymes**
    1 year, 23
    3 years, 64
    5 years, 85, 89–90
    kindergarten readiness checklist, 93

N
Nine-month-old milestones, 14–15
9 to 12 months, 18–20
Nonverbal feedback, 59
Numbers. *See* **Counting and numbers**
Nutrition, 32, 101

O
Oedipal behavior, 73
1-year-old milestones, 21–22
Outside playtime
    3 years, 65–66
    4 years, 72, 80
    5 years, 90, 98

P
Parents
    cell phone distractions and, iv–v, 16–17, 32, 99
    common mistakes of, 98–100
    positive parenting tips, 50–51, 59, 73–74
    staying calm, 56
    temperament of, 29
    training children's brains for success, 101–4
Pat-A-Cake, 25
Patience
    frustrations of child and, 73–75
    learning self-control and, 40
    learning to share, 29
    potty training and, 49
    sleep schedules and, 12
    Why? questions, 58
Patterns, 65
Physical milestones. *See* **Movement/ physical milestones**
Picky eaters, 29

Play dates, 59, 84
Positive affirmations, 74–75
Positive parenting behavior tips, 50–51, 59, 73–74
Potty training, 49
Praise
    12 months, 23
    18 months, 41
    24 to 30 months, 50–51, 55
    30 to 36 months, 64
    4 years, 74
    5 years, 84
    positive self-affirmations and, 74–75
    potty training and, 49
    training children's brains for success and, 101
Premature babies, 8, 43
Preschool, 72
Pretend play
    18 to 24 months, 39, 41–42
    24 to 30 months, 48, 56–57
    4 years, 72
    5 years, 85
Problem solving
    15 to 18 months, 34–35
    18 to 24 months, 39, 41
    24 to 30 months, 57
    30 to 36 months, 58, 59
    5 years, 84
Prooday, Victoria, 68, 98
Punishments. *See* **Discipline**

R
Radiation from cell phones, v
Reading. *See also* **Alphabet**
    3 to 6 months, 6
    9 to 12 months, 19, 23
    12 to 15 months, 28, 31
    15 to 18 months, 34
    18 to 24 months, 39, 41
    24 to 30 months, 55
    30 to 36 months, 62
    4 years, 72, 78
    5 years, 84–85, 88
    kindergarten readiness checklist, 91
    nursery rhymes, memorization of, 65
    pattern skills and, 65
Regression, 54
Reset Your Child's Brain **(Dunckley),** 67
Respiratory symptoms and infections, 17
Responsive care, ii
Rewards vs. punishments, 20, 41, 49, 59. *See also* **Praise**
Right handedness, 89
Rock-a-Bye Baby, 25
Rolling over, 6
Routines
    3 to 6 months, 6
    30 to 36 months, 62
    for bedtime, 13, 29, 62
    consistency of, 101
    for goodbyes, 13, 18, 20
Rules and consequences, 31, 40, 62, 74, 101

S
Safety. *See also* **Childproofing; Screen time**
    12 to 15 months, 32–33
    24 to 30 months, 50
    brain development and, ii
    secondhand smoke and, 17
    sexuality education and, 73
School readiness
    chores and, 88
    cooperation and friendliness, 59
    following directions, 88
    games for, 63–64
    kindergarten readiness checklist, 91–94
    reading to children and, 6, 62
    screen time and, 16
Scissors and cutting activities, 64
Screen time
    AAP recommendations for children, 16, 32
    as babysitter, 99

Index

cell phone distracted parenting and, iv–v, 16–17, 32, 99
cell phone radiation and, v
digital media and the brain, 67–69
replacing outside playtime, 98
training children's brains for success and, 101
Secondhand smoke, 17
Self-awareness, 35
Self-confidence, 24, 88, 102
Self-control, 29, 39, 40, 69, 94
Self-knowledge, 93
Self-soothing
    birth to 3 months, 2
    3 to six months, 12
Sensory play, 42
Separation anxiety, 13, 20
Sexuality, questions about, 73
Shapes identification, 64
Sharing and turn taking
    12 to 15 months, 29
    2 years, 56
    24 to 30 months, 48
    30 to 36 months, 58, 59, 63
    5 years, 90
    kindergarten readiness checklist, 93
Shelter resources, 131–33
Sibling relationships, 59
SIDS (sudden infant death syndrome), 17
6-month-old milestones, 10–11
6 to 9 months, 12–13
Sleep
    3 to 6 months, 6
    6 to 9 months, 12–13
    bedtime routines and, 13, 29, 62
Smart phones. *See* **Screen time**
Smoking, 17
Social/emotional milestones
    4 months, 8
    6 months, 10
    9 months, 14
    1 year, 21
    18 months, 37
    2 years, 43
    30 months, 52
    3 years, 60
    4 years, 76
    5 years, 86
Social skills. *See also* **Friends**
    12 to 15 months, 29
    24 to 30 months, 48
    30 to 36 months, 59
    5 years, 84, 85, 90
    cell phone distracted parenting and, 16–17
    screen time and, 69
    teaching, 98–99, 102
Songs and nursery rhymes
    9 to 12 months, 19, 24–25
    15 to 18 months, 34
    18 to 24 months, 42
    30 to 36 months, 65
Sorting games, 39
Spanking, 20
Spoiling children, ii, 2, 7
Sports participation, 84
Stair safety, 32
Storytelling, 72, 78, 89
Sudden infant death syndrome (SIDS), 17
Swaddling, 3
Swimming pools, 32

T
Talking. *See* **Language and conversation**
Tantrums
    15 to 18 months, 34
    24 to 30 months, 48, 50, 53
Teaching tips
    birth to 3 months, 3–4
    3 to 6 months, 7
    6 to 9 months, 13
    9 to 12 months, 19–20, 23–25
    12 to 15 months, 31–32
    18 to 24 months, 41–42
    24 to 30 months, 55–57

30 to 36 months, 59, 62–66
4 years, 78–80
5 years, 88–90
cell phone distracted parenting and, 16–17, 32
responsive care and, ii
training children's brains for success, 101–4

Teeth
brushing, 55
night feedings and health of, 13
teething, 30

Televisions. *See* **Screen time**
Temperament, 28–29
Temperature, method for taking, 4
Terrasse, Isabelle, 67
30 to 36 months, 58–66
30-month milestones, 52–54
3 year milestones, 60–61
teaching tips for, 62–66

3 to 6 months, 6–7
Time, understanding, 19, 78–79
Time Magazine **on cell phone-distracted parenting, 16**
Time-outs, 20, 62
Tobacco smoke, 17
Toilet training, 49
Transitions, 79
Trust
birth to 3 months, 2
cell phone distracted parenting and, iv–v
child's fears, responding to, 48
goodbye routines, 13, 18

Turn taking. *See* **Sharing and turn taking**
12-month-old milestones, 21–22
12 to 15 months, 28–33
24 to 30 months, 48–57
24-month milestones, 43–44
30-month milestones, 52–53
common behaviors, 53–54
positive parenting behavior tips, 50–51
teaching tips for, 55–57
toilet training, 49

Twinkle, Twinkle Little Star, 25
2-year-old milestones, 43–44

V
Values, 102–3
Video games. *See* **Screen time**
Vocabulary, building
9 to 12 months, 19
18 to 24 months, 40
30 to 36 months, 58, 65
4 years, 72, 78
5 years, 88

W
Walking
12 to 15 months, 28
15-month milestones, 30
15 to 18 months, 34
24 to 30 months, 48

Water safety, 32
Weather, 65–66
Writing. *See also* **Alphabet**
12 months, 23
30 to 36 months, 58
4 years, 72
5 years, 84–85, 89
kindergarten readiness checklist, 92

CPSIA information can be obtained
at www.ICGtesting.com
Printed in the USA
JSHW040806190420
5124JS00001B/1